Ontario Lighthouses

by Harold Stiver

Copyright Statement

Ontario Lighthouses
A Guide for Photographers and Explorers

Published by Harold Stiver

Version 1.0
ISBN: 978-1-927835-28-9

Contents

A Short History of Lighthouses Page 7
The Imperial Towers 9
Central Ontario Region Lighthouses
Badgeley Island 11
Cabot Head 12
Cape Croker 13
Flowerpot Island 14
Gereaux Island 15
Griffith Island 16
Killarney East 17
Killarney Northwest 17
Pointe au Baril Range Front 18
Pointe au Baril Range Rear 18
Red Rock 19
Snug Harbour Range Rear 20
Walton Island Range Front 20
Victoria Harbour Range Rear 21
Western Islands 22
Other Central Ontario Region Lighthouses 23
Beausoleil Island, Brébeuf Island, Bustard Rocks, Bustard Rocks Range, Byng Inlet Range Front, Byng Inlet Range Rear, Cape Robert, Cecebe Lake, Christian Island, French River Range, Giants Tomb Island, Gravenhurst Narrows (Lighthouse Island), Jones Island Range Front, Jones Island Range Rear, Rosseau (Lighthouse Shoal), Southeast Bay, Spruce Shoal, Wilson Channel Range Front, Wilson Channel Range Rear

Eastern Ontario Region Lighthouses
Cape North 27
Cobourg East Pierhead 28
De Watteville Island Ranges 29
Deep River Islet 30
Dickinson Landing 31
McQuestin Point 32
Point Petre 33
Prescott Heritage Harbour 34
Prescott 35
Presqu'île Point 36
Windmill Point 37
Other Eastern Ontario Region Lighthouses 38
False Ducks, False Ducks 1967, Knapp Point, L'Orignal Range Front, L'Orignal Range Rear, Lancaster Range, Main Duck, Morris Island (Victoria Island), Nine Mile Point, Pigeon Island, Prince Edward Point, Salmon Point, Sand Point, Scotch Bonnet Island, Wolfe Island (Québec Head)

Golden Horseshoe Region Lighthouses
Burlington Canal Main 41
Burlington Canal Pier 41
Gibraltar Point 43
Mohawk Island 44
Niagara River Range Front 45
Niagara River Range Rear 45
Oakville 47
Point Abino 48
Port Credit (replica) 50
Port Dalhousie Range Front 51
Port Dalhousie Range Rear 51
Port Weller 53
Queen's Wharf 54
Toronto Harbour 55
Other Golden Horseshoe Region Lighthouses 56
Port Colborne Inner, Port Colborne Outer, Toronto East Entrance Inner, Toronto East Entrance Outer

Northwestern Ontario Region Lighthouses
Battle Island 57
Caribou Island 58
Gros Cap Reefs 59
Ile Parisienne 60
Janet Head (Gore Bay) 61
Kagawong 62
Manitowaning 63
Michipicoten Island East End 64
Mississagi Strait 65
Thunder Bay Main 66
Other Northwestern Ontario Region Lighthouses 67
Angus Island, Coppermine Point, Corbeil Point, Davieaux Island, Great Duck Island, Lamb Island, Little Current, Lonely Island, McKay Island, Michael's Bay, Michipicoten Harbour, Otter Island, Pie Island, Pointe aux Pins Range Front, Pointe aux Pins Range Rear, Porphyry Point, Providence Bay, Shaganash (Island No. 10), Shoal Island, Slate Islands, South Baymouth Range Front, South Baymouth Range Rear, Strawberry Island, Tomahawk Island, Trowbridge Island, Welcome Island, West Sister Rock

Southwestern Ontario Region Lighthouses
Big Tub (Tobermory) 73
Bois Blanc Island 75
Chantry Island 76
Cove Island 78
Goderich 79

Grand Bend 80
Kincardine 81
Lion's Head 82
Long Point Cut 84
Long Point 85
Pelee Island 87
Point Clark 88
Port Burwell 89
Port Dover 90
Port Maitland 91
Thames River Range Rear 92
Other Southwestern Ontario Region Lighthouses 93
Colchester Reef, Corunna Range Rear, Goderich Breakwater, Kingsville, Leamington, McNab Point, Midland Point Range Front, Midland Point Range Rear, Nancy Island (replica), Nottawasaga, Pelee Passage, Pelee Passage New, Point Edward Range, Port Burwell Entrance, Port Stanley, Rondeau East Pier, Rondeau West Breakwater, Saugeen River Range Front, Saugeen River Range Rear, Southeast Shoal, Stokes Bay Range Front, Stokes Bay Range Rear

Tours
Lake Erie Lighthouse Tour 98
Golden Horseshoe Lighthouse Tour 99
Lake Ontario Lighthouse Tour 100
Manitoulin Lighthouse Tour 101
Lake Huron Lighthouse Tour 102

Glossary of Lighthouse Terms 103
Photo Credits 107
Other Books by Harold Stiver 108
Index 109

A Short History of Lighthouses

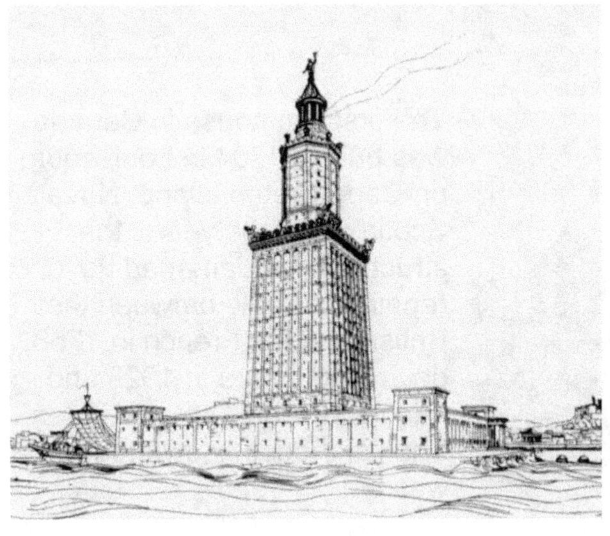

There is some evidence of a lighthouse from the 5th century B.C. of Themistocles of Athens constructing a stone column with a fire on top. This was at the harbour of Piraeus, associated with Athens.

However one of most famous and spectacular early structures was the Lighthouse of Alexandria, or the Pharos of Alexandria. It was one of the Seven Wonders of the Ancient World.

The lighthouse was built in the Third Century B.C. in Alexandria, Egypt by Ptolemy II. It stood on the island of Pharos in the harbour of Alexandria and was said to be 110 metres (350 feet) high.

The lighthouse was built in three stages, a large square at the bottom, an octagonal layer in the middle, and a cylindrical tower at the top.

The structure lasted until a series of earthquakes damaged it, with the 1303 Crete earthquake resulting in its destruction.

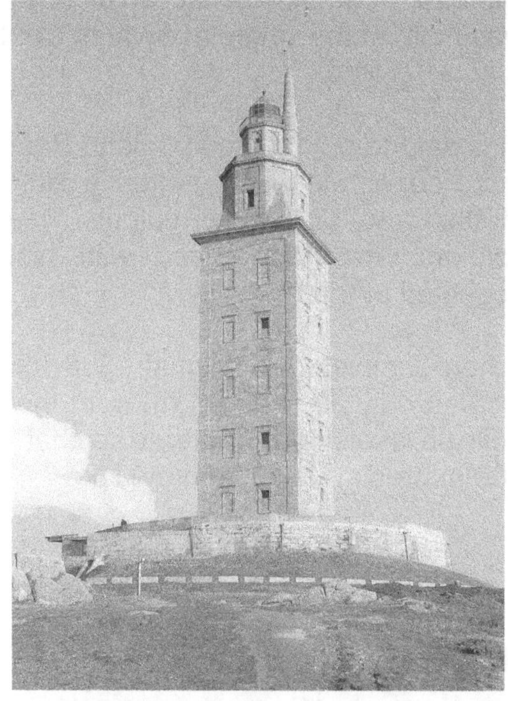

The Tower of Hercules, in northwest Spain, is modeled after the Pharos Lighthouse.

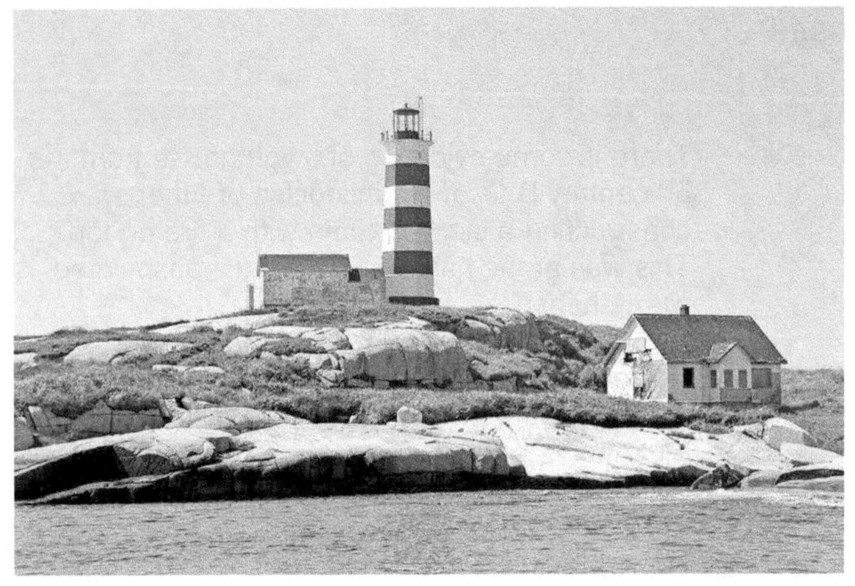

The first lighthouse in Canada was built in 1734 in Louisbourg on Cape Breton Island, Nova Scotia. Over the years, the structure was damaged beyond repair in a battle between the British and the French in 1758, destroyed by fire in 1923 and had to be rebuilt several times. The lighthouse known today was built in 1923.

Currently Canada's oldest surviving lighthouse is Sambro Island Lighthouse, built in 1758 at the entrance to Halifax Harbour. It is seen in the image above.

The oldest surviving lighthouse in Ontario is the Gibraltar Point Lighthouse which opened in 1808. It was built at the southern point of Centre Island, in the City of Toronto.

It is said to be haunted by John Paul Radelmuller, the first Keeper. He was apparently murdered on the 2nd of January, 1815. The culprits were thought to be soldiers who had argued with him but they were acquitted at trial.

When completed in August 1808, the lighthouse was located only 25 feet (7.6 m) from the shore. Sand has built up over time, however so that it now sits about 100 metres (110 yd) from the lake.

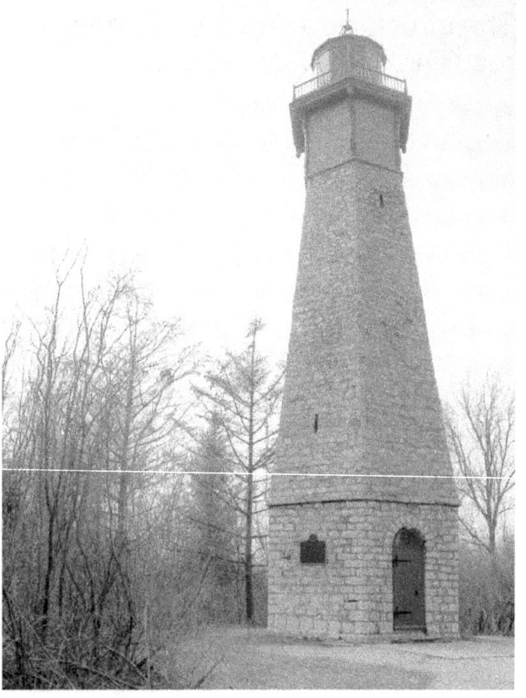

The Imperial Towers

In 1853, the Commissioners of Public Works reported on the necessity of providing lighthouses to guide ships on Lake Huron. The area was increasingly being settled and commercial enterprises expanding to this area. Shipping was increasing to service this activity.

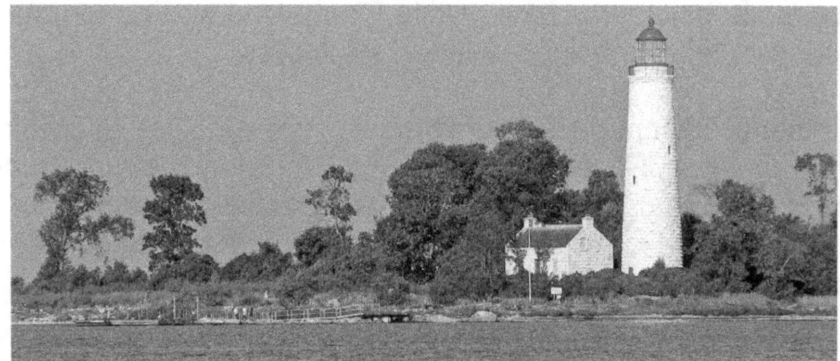

Chantry Island Lighthouse

With input from Ship's Captains and other interested parties, the Commissioners decided to have eleven lighthouses constructed and in 1855 the project was tendered. John Brown, a builder from Thorold, was contracted to build these eleven lighthouses as well as Keepers' dwellings. Brown had already completed his first government lighthouse project at Mohawk Island in Lake Erie in 1848 as well as other government projects and he had an excellent reputation for meticulous work. The proposed lighthouses were to be built at:

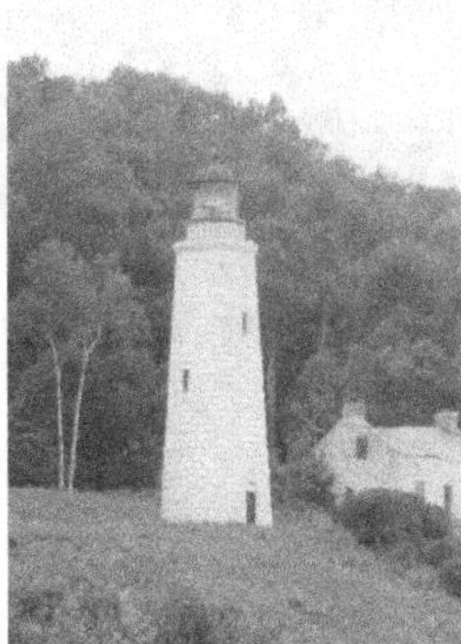

Griffith Island

1. Point Clark
2. Chantry Island
3. Cove Island
4. Nottawasaga Island
5. Griffith Island
6. Christian Island
7. White Fish Island
8. Mississagi Strait
9. Isle St. Joseph
10. Clapperton Island
11. Badgley Island

It soon became apparent that the original contract price of 3,500 pounds was going to be inadequate as the logistics and scope of the project became a nightmare. Brown had white dolomite limestone quarries opened and arranged shipment to the sites. However storms and natural hazards created havoc and four of the supply ships were lost. Additionally the Fresnel lighting apparatus made in France was delayed due to high demand.

Brown was losing money on the project which couldn't be sustained and he petitioned the government for relief. Eventually only the first six lighthouses were built and Brown seems to have weathered the financial crisis. Cove Island, Nottawasaga Island and Griffith Island Lighthouses opened in 1858 and Chantry Island, Point Clark and Christian Island Lighthouses in 1959. The standards Brown used were of the highest and all of the stations are still active. Of the five lighthouses not built at the time, White Fish Island was never built while the rest were completed later with less ambitious wooden structures.

There were other Imperial Towers outside of Ontario. These include at Lotbinière, Quebec, Pointe-aux-Trembles, Quebec, L'Islet, Quebec, Lake St. Peter, Isle aux Prunes opposite Verchères, Quebec which were all built in the 1860s. Also they were built for the St Lawrence River approaches at Cap-des-Rosiers on the Gaspe, the Strait of Belle Isle, Pointe Amour on the Labrador coast and at West Point on Anticosti Island

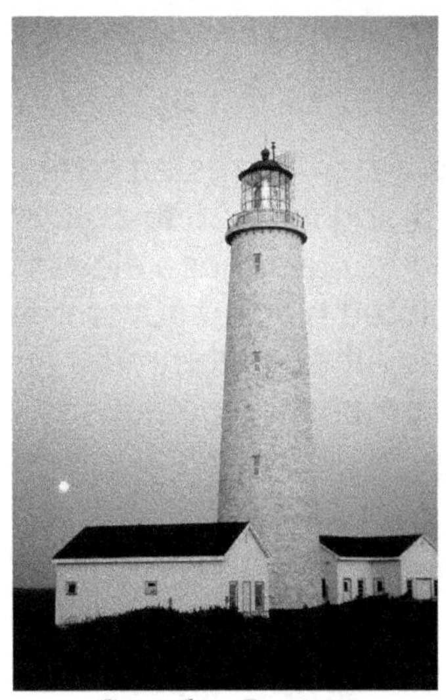

Cap-des-Rosiers Lighthouse, Quebec

Badgeley Island Lighthouse, Central Ontario Region

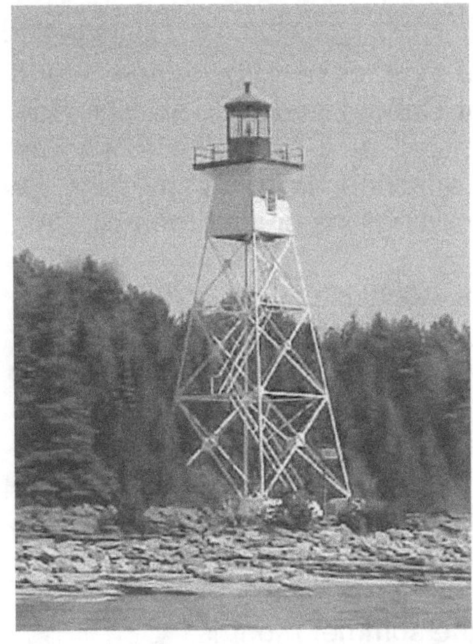

A lighthouse was proposed for Badgeley Island as early as the 1850s to protect shipping using the North Channel on Lake Huron. However it was not until 1912 that a pair of range lights were built.

The range lights were demolished in 1981, when the present tower was built.

Description: Skeleton tower with red top

Location: Badgeley Island

Directions: Accessible by boat

Coordinates: 45°55'43.2"N 81°36'09.3"W

Opened: 1981

Automated: 1981

Deactivated: Active

Height: 30 feet (9.2 metres)

Focal Height: 42 feet (12.9 metres)

Signal: White flash each 4 seconds

Visitor Access: Grounds open, interior closed

Cabot Head Lighthouse, Central Ontario Region

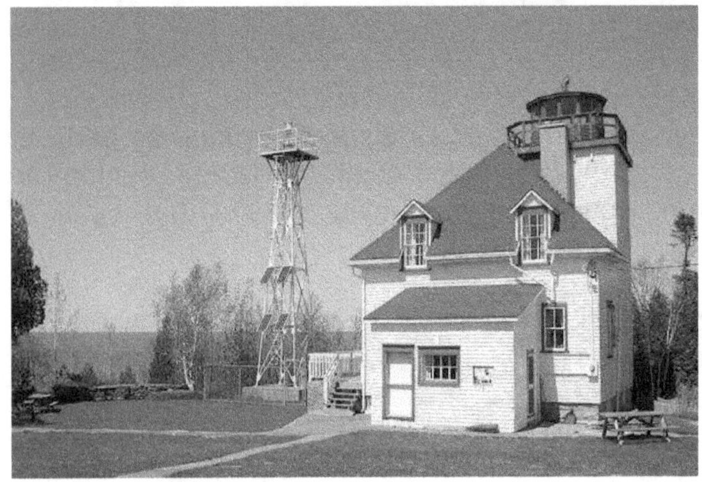

In 1896 a lighthouse with foghorn alarm opened at Cabot Head on Georgian Bay. This consisted of a forty-nine foot tower and an attached keepers dwelling. A foghorn building was erected nearby.

The light consisted of a parabolic reflectors and lamps. It was set at eighty feet above the bay. The foghorn building was destroyed in a fire in 1907 but was quickly replaced. In 1929 the light was replaced and produced a single white flash every twenty-five seconds

In 1971 a skeleton tower replaced the lighthouse. A local group of volunteers have renovated the old lighthouse and it is available for visitors in the summer months.

Description: White skeleton tower

Location: Dyer's Bay

Directions: From Dyers Bay head northeast on Dyers Bay Rd toward for 1.9 km and turn right onto Birch Rd. After 350 m, turn right onto Shoreline Dr and in 350 m, turn right onto Cabot Head Rd. You will find the lighthouse in 8 km.

Coordinates: 45°14'42.4"N 81°17'31.7"W

Opened: 1971

Automated: 1971

Deactivated: Active

Height: 42 feet (12.9 metres)

Focal Height: 79 feet (24.1 metres)

Signal: White flash every 10 seconds

Visitor Access: Grounds open, interior open May through October

Cape Croker Lighthouse, Central Ontario Region

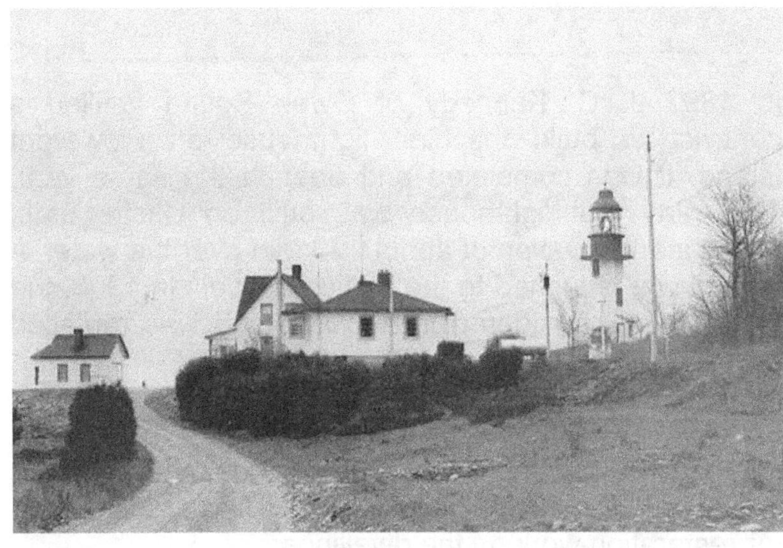

In 1902 a light and fog alarm was established at Cape Croker on Georgian Bay.

In 1909 the current lighthouse tower was completed, standing 15.9 metres tall. It was equipped with a third-order, Fresnel lens. The fog alarm was upgraded in 1927.

The residence and foghorn building were removed in 1975.

Description: White octagonal tower, red lantern

Location: Cape Croker

Directions: From Cape Croker, head NW on Pit Rd for 1.1 km and turn left onto Wilmer's Rd. Proceed for 1.0 km and turn right onto Lighthouse Rd where you find the lighthouse in 6.7 km

Coordinates: 44°57'21.4"N 80°57'37.4"W

Opened: 1909

Automated: 1886

Deactivated: Active

Lens: Third-order Fresnel

Height: 53 feet (15.9 metres)

Focal Height: 61 feet (18.7 metres)

Signal: White flash for two seconds followed by 2 second pause

Foghorn signal: 15 second blast followed by 15 second eclipse

Visitor Access: Grounds open, interior closed

Flowerpot Island Lighthouse, Central Ontario Region

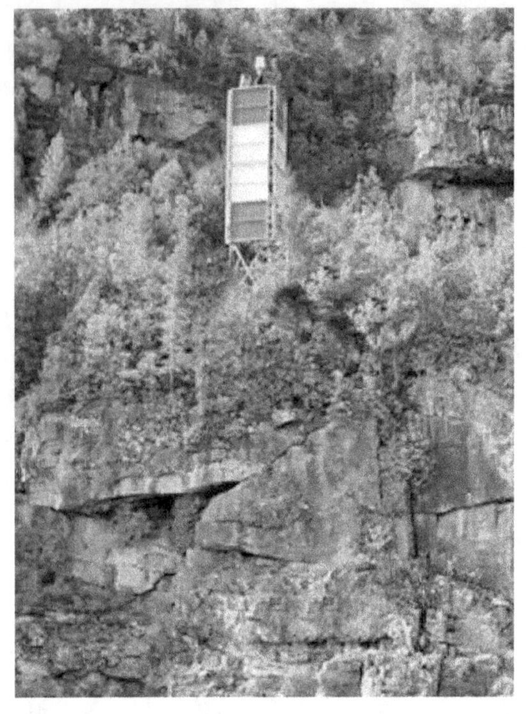

In 1897 J. C. Kennedy of Owen Sound fulfilled a contract to build the first lighthouse on Flowerpot Island. It was completed and opened the same year. The thirty foot lighthouse was built on Castle Bluff, giving it an elevation of about 120 feet over the water. A fogbell was attached to the station as well. In 1908, the fogbell was considered inadequate and was replaced by a diaphone plant.

In 1968 the lighthouse was replaced by the current steel tower pyramid. The old lighthouse tower was destroyed. The Friends of Fathom Five have arranged for restoration work on the dwellings.

The station was listed as a Historic Place on May 29, 2015. This included the following buildings: (1) the 1963 Boathouse, (2) the 1901 Lightkeeper's Dwelling, (3) the 1959 Assistant Lightkeeper's Dwelling, and (4) the Observation Deck Building

Description: Square tower, white daymark

Location: Flowerpot Island

Directions: Take the tour boat from Tobermory

Coordinates: 45°18'25.9"N 81°36'49.6"W

Opened: 1968

Automated: 1968

Deactivated: Active

Focal Height: 124 feet (27.7 metres)

Signal: White flash every 10 seconds

Visitor Access: Grounds open, interior closed

Gereaux Island Lighthouse, Central Ontario Region

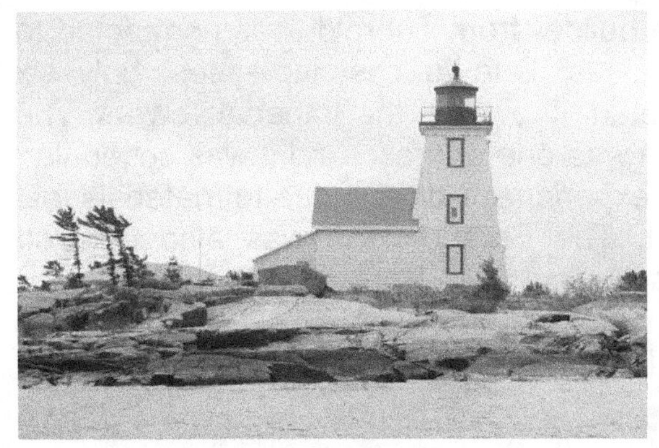

In 1869 the Magnetawan River area around Byng Inlet was experiencing growth primarily due to lumber production. Lumber was shipped through Georgian Bay, at the mouth of the river. Lumber companies suggested to the government that a lighthouse was needed there and and that they would pay half of the cost. This first lighthouse on Gereaux Island was eventually built and opened in 1870.

By 1878 the Department of Marine, who were now in charge of the station, did an inspection. They found it was in very poor condition and recommended it be replaced. Parliament agreed to this in 1879 and the new Lighthouse opened in 1880. In 1911, a fourth-order Fresnel lens was installed

The Lighthouse and Dwelling were listed as a Federal Heritage Building on July 11, 2008

Description: Square, pyramidal tower

Location: Byng Inlet

Directions: Accessible by boat

Coordinates: 45°44'39.8"N 80°39'32.4"W

Opened: 1880

Automated: 1989

Deactivated: Active

Height: 50 feet (15.1 metres)

Focal Height: 52 feet (15.9 metres)

Signal: Occulting white light, 10 seconds

Foghorn Signal: Blast 7 seconds, eclipse 3 seconds

Visitor Access: No access to tower

Griffith Island Lighthouse, Central Ontario Region

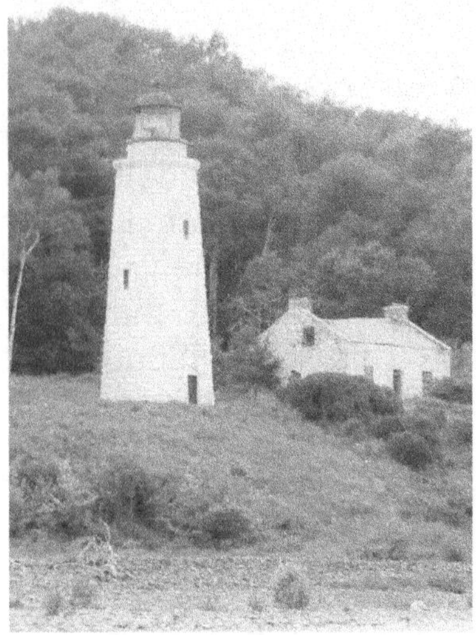

In 1855, John Brown, a builder from Thorold, was contracted to construct eleven lighthouses. Due to cost increases, only six lighthouses were completed, known as the Imperial Towers. The Griffith Island Lighthouse was one of these and it was scheduled for early completion but experienced delays due to materials lost at sea during transport. The Fresnel lens was also delayed from the French manufacturers.

You can read about the Imperial Towers in a separate article on page 9.

it was completed and opened in 1858. It operated with a third-order Fresnel lens, then state of the art.

Description: White cylindrical tower with red lantern room

Location: Griffith Island in Georgian Bay

Directions: Accessible by boat

Coordinates: 44°51'02.1"N 80°53'28.3"W

Opened: 1858

Automated: 1924

Deactivated: Active

Lens: Third-order Fresnel

Height: 64 feet (19.5 metres)

Focal Height: 102 feet (31.3 metres)

Signal: White flash every 4 seconds.

Visitor Access: Grounds open, interior closed

Killarney Lighthouses, Central Ontario Region

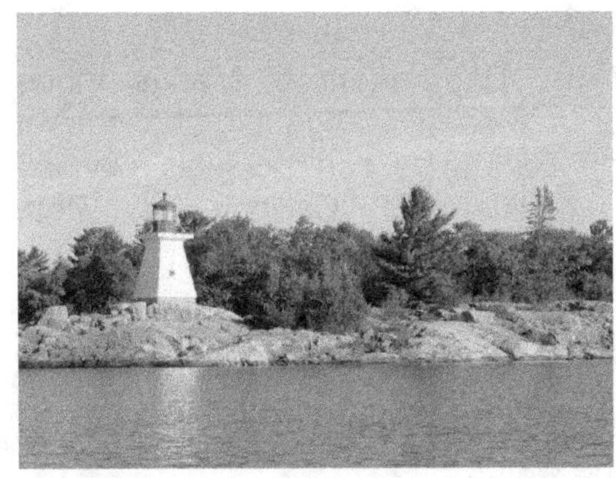

In the 1850's, a contract was given to John Brown of Thorold to build eleven lighthouses on Georgian Bay and Lake Huron including one at Killarney. However only six of these were built due to budget restraints. Killarney was not one of them and it wasn't until 1866 before the two Killarney lighthouses were built. The six lighthouses built became known as the Imperial Lighthouses. The present lighthouses, Killarney Northwest and Killarney East, were opened in 1909.

In 1950, the keepers at Badgeley Island Lighthouse, Ferdinand and Merle Solomon, changed places with the Killarney keeper, Frank Sinclair. This took place after the couple's young son drowned, and they wanted to be close to their other children who where at school in Killarney.

Killarney East

Description: White square tower

Location: Partridge Island

Directions: Accessible by boat

Coordinates: 45°59'02.2"N 81°31'55.8"W

Opened: 1909

Automated: N/A

Deactivated: Active

Height: 29 feet (8.9 metres)

Focal Height: 40 feet (12.3 metres)

Signal: White light, two sec on, two sec off

Visitor Access: Grounds open, interior closed

Killarney Northwest

Description: Red and white cylindrical tower

Location: Killarney

Directions: From ON-637, head SW on Ontario St and after 0.9 km, continue on Lighthouse Rd for 0.9 km where you find the lighthouse

Coordinates: 45°58'05.4"N 81°29'19.9"W

Opened: 1909

Automated: 1982

Deactivated: Active

Height: 30 feet (9.1 metres)

Focal Height: 56 feet (17.1 metres)

Signal: White flash every 4 seconds

Visitor Access: Grounds open, interior closed

Pointe au Baril Range Lighthouses, Central Ontario Region

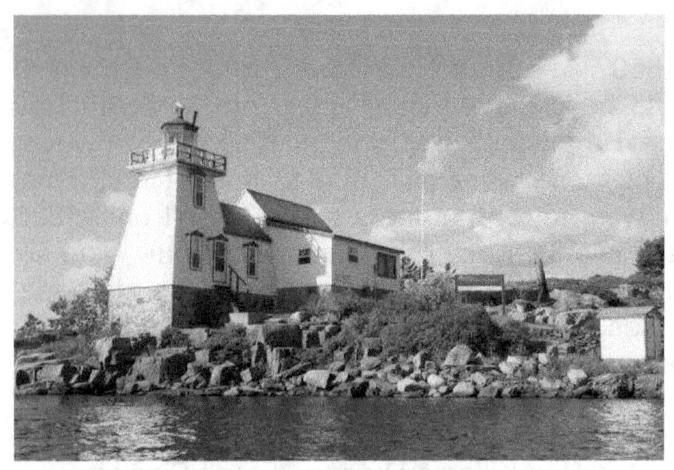

In 1887 the Department of Marine made plans for a pair of Range Lighthouses at Pointe au Baril. The contract was won by Charles Mickler, of Collingwood. Both stations opened in 1889.

The Front Range Light is a square tower painted white with a dwelling for the Keeper. It is located on the southern tip of the point next to the water.
The Rear Range Light was initially a open frame square tower of 44 feet. In 1903 it was replaced by a steel tower of sixty-one feet with an enclosed lantern room at the top. To increase the visibility this was replaced by a ninety-three foot steel tower in 1909. The Front Range Light was listed as a Federal Heritage Building on July 11, 2008.

	Front Range	**Rear Range**
Description:	White square tower	White skeleton tower
Location:	Pointe au Baril	Macklin Island
Directions:	Accessible by boat	Accessible by boat
Coordinates:	45°33'32.9"N 80°30'12.7"W	45°33'09.7"N 80°29'15.7"W
Opened:	1889	1909
Automated:	1983	1909
Deactivated:	Active	Active
Lens:	Dioptric	
Height:	32 feet (9.7 metres)	61 feet (19 metres)
Focal Height:	38 feet (11.6 metres)	93 feet (28 metres)
Signal:	Fixed Red	Fixed Red

Visitor Access: Grounds open, interior open in season

Red Rock Lighthouse, Central Ontario Region

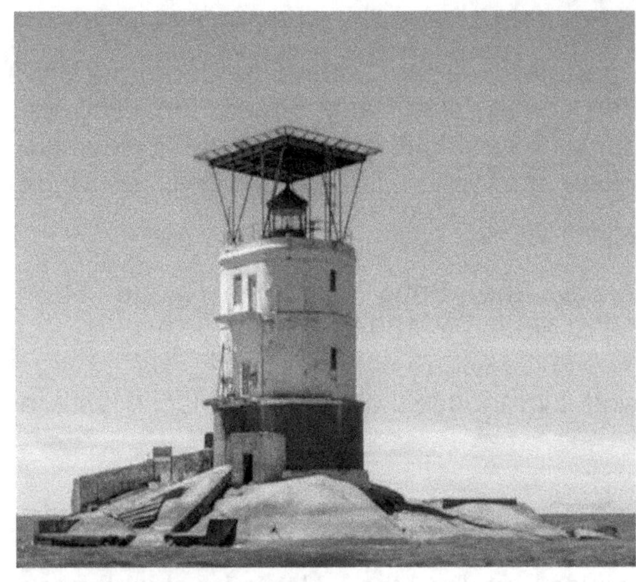

The first lighthouse on Red Rock opened in 1881, and served to protect shipping bound for Parry Sound. It was an octagonal tower rising from the roof of the keepers dwelling. In 1905, the light was upgraded with a fourth-order Fresnel lens.

The present Red Rock Lighthouse opened in 1912. A diaphone fog alarm plant was added the next year.

Red Rock Lighthouse was listed as a Recognized Federal Heritage Building on July 24, 2009

Description: Red and white cylindrical tower

Location: Carling

Directions: Accessible by boat

Coordinates: 45°21'36.0"N 80°24'29.0"W

Opened: 1912

Automated: 1977

Deactivated: Active

Lens: Fourth-order Fresnel

Height: 60 feet (18.3 metres)

Focal Height: 62 feet (19 metres)

Signal: White flash every 4 seconds

Visitor Access: Closed

Snug Harbour Range Lighthouses, Central Ontario Region

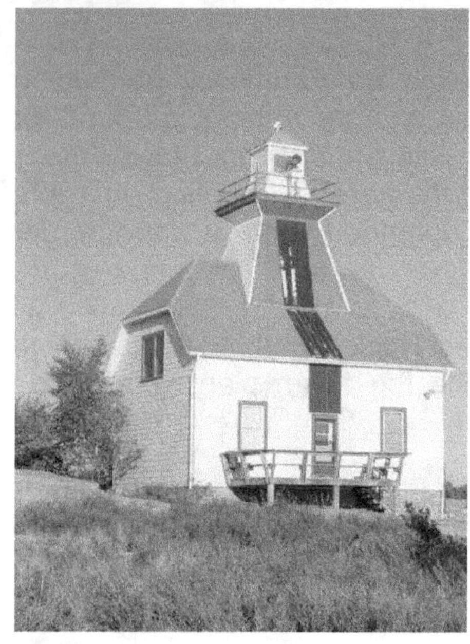

In 1891 the Department of the Marine tendered for five lighthouses for the channels to Parry Sound, including the Snug Harbour Range Rear Lighthouse. It would work with a proposed lighthouse on Walton Island as a pair of range lights.

After some delays, the Snug Harbour Range Rear Lighthouse began operating in 1894.

The Walton Island Lighthouse has been replaced with a skeleton tower.

Snug Harbour Rear Range Lighthouse was designated as a Recognized Federal Heritage Building in 2007, as a Heritage Lighthouse under the Heritage Lighthouse Protection Act In 2016.

Snug Harbour Range Rear

Description: White square tower, red upper

Location: Snug Island

Directions: Accessible by boat

Coordinates: 45°22'25.6"N 80°18'40.5"W

Opened: 1894

Automated: Ca. 1932

Deactivated: Active

Height: 48 feet (14.7 metres)

Focal Height: 57 feet (17.5 metres)

Signal: Fixed Green

Visitor Access: Closed

Walton Island Range Front

Description: Skeleton tower

Location: Walton Island

Directions: Accessible by boat

Coordinates: 45°22'15"N 80°19'19"W

Deactivated: Active

Height: 23 feet (7 metres)

Focal Height: 39 feet (11.8 metres)

Signal: Fixed Green

Visitor Access: Closed

Victoria Harbour Range Rear Lighthouse, Central Ontario Region

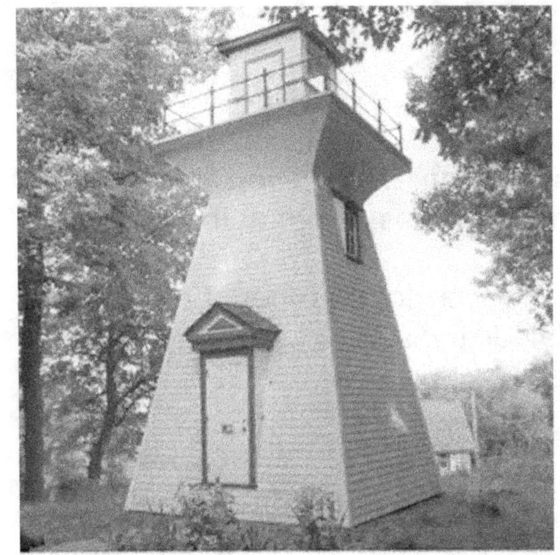

In 1910, the Department of Marine built two wooden lighthouses at Victoria Harbour. The front tower was replaced by a skeleton tower in 1960.

The range was discontinued in 1990.

Tay Township Heritage Committee took ownership of the rear tower in 2004 and arranged restoration of the lighthouse. A re-opening was held in 2012.

Description: Square tower

Location: Victoria Harbour

Directions: 283 William St, Victoria Harbour

Coordinates: 44°44'48.9"N 79°46'37.2"W

Opened: 1910

Automated: 1951

Deactivated: 1990s

Height: 45 feet (13.5 metres)

Focal Height: 150 feet (45.6 metres)

Signal: Fixed green

Visitor Access: Grounds open, interior closed

Western Islands Lighthouse, Central Ontario Region

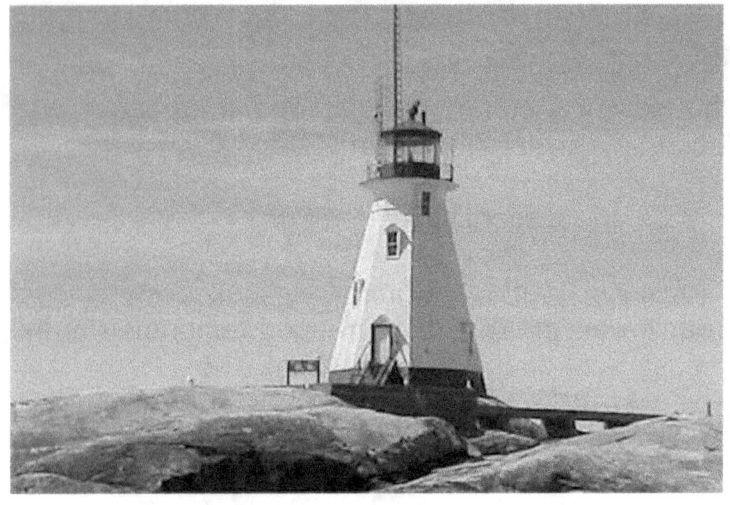

In 1895 the Western Islands Lighthouse was built on Double Top Island. A fog alarm plant was added at that time.

In 1896 a fourth-order Fresnel lens updated the Dioptric of the seventh order.

In 1919 the fog alarm plant was replaced with a diaphone foghorn.

Description: White octagonal tower

Location: Double Top Island

Directions: Accessible by boat

Coordinates: 45°02'11.9"N 80°21'14.3"W

Opened: 1895

Automated: 1967

Deactivated: Active

Lens: Fourth-order Fresnel

Height: 50 feet (15.2 metres)

Focal Height: 74 feet (22.6 metres)

Signal: White flash every 10 seconds

Foghorn Signal: Three-second blast every thirty seconds

Visitor Access: Closed

Other Central Ontario Region Lighthouses

Name: Beausoleil Island
Description: Skeletal tower
Directions: Accessible by boat
Automated: 1962
Height: 52 feet (15.8 metres)
Coordinates: 44°52'36.9"N 79°52'28.9"W
Location: Beausoleil Island
Opened: 1915
Lens: Reflectors
Access: Grounds open, interior closed

Name: Brébeuf Island
Description: White cylindrical tower
Directions: Accessible by boat
Automated: 1962
Height: 36 feet (11 metres)
Signal: White flash of 2 sec, 2 sec eclipse
Coordinates: 44°52'36.1"N 79°53'04.1"W
Location: Brébeuf Island
Opened: 1900
Deactivated: Active
Focal Height: 40 feet (12.1 metres)
Access: Closed

Name: Bustard Rocks Lighthouse
Description: Square, white tower
Directions: Accessible by boat
Automated: 1999
Lens: Catoptric
Focal Height: 48 feet (14.6 metres)
Access: Grounds open, interior closed
Coordinates: 45°53'27.1"N 80°57'07.7"W
Location: Bustard Rocks
Opened: 1893
Deactivated: Active
Height: 39 feet (11.9 metres)
Signal: White flash every 10 seconds

Name: Bustard Rocks Range
Description: Square, skeleton tower
Directions: Accessible by boat
Automated: 1951
Lens: Catoptric
Signal: Fixed red
Coordinates: 45°53'30.1"N 80°57'05.9"W
Location: Bustard Rocks
Opened: 1914
Deactivated: 1999
Height: 37 feet (11.2 metres)
Access: Grounds open, interior closed

Name: Byng Inlet Range Front
Description: White tower, orange stripe
Directions: Accessible by boat
Automated: 1989
Height: 33 feet (10.1 metres)
Signal: Fixed red
Coordinates: 45°45'09.0"N 80°38'42.8"W
Location: Britt
Opened: 1936
Deactivated: Active
Focal Height: 38 feet (11.6 metres)
Access: Grounds open, interior closed

Name: Byng Inlet Range Rear
Description: White skeleton tower
Directions: Accessible by boat
Automated: 1989
Height: 47 feet (14.4 metres)
Signal: Fixed red
Coordinates: 45°45'09.4"N 80°38'26.9"W
Location: Britt
Opened: 1936
Deactivated: Active
Focal Height: 57 feet (17.4 metres)
Access: Grounds open, interior closed

Name: Cape Robert
Coordinates: 45°20'40.7"N 80°02'31.1"W
Description: Lantern room used as entrance to Canadian Coast Guard building
Location: Parry Sound
Directions: 28 Waubeek St, Parry Sound
Opened: 1885
Automated: 1957
Deactivated: Ca.1970
Height: 41 feet (12.5 metres)
Focal Height: 46 feet (14 metres)
Signal: Fixed white
Access: Grounds open, interior closed

Name: Cecebe Lake
Coordinates: 45°40'02.6"N 79°37'26.5"W
Description: Square tapering tower
Location: Magnetawan River
Directions: From Magnetawan, go east on Borrows Road for 1.6 km and the lighthouse on river to the south
Opened: 2022
Deactivated: Never active (Replica)
Height: 23 feet (7 metres)
Access: Grounds open, interior closed

Name: Christian Island
Coordinates: 44°47'11.9"N 80°09'21.8"W
Description: White cylindrical tower
Location: Christian Island
Directions: Accessible by ferry
Opened: 1859
Deactivated: 1922
Lens: Fourth-order Fresnel
Height: 57 feet (17.5 metres)
Focal Height: 66 feet (20.2 metres)
Signal: White flash every 4 seconds
Foghorn Signal: Blast every 10 seconds
Access: Grounds open, interior closed

Name: French River Range
Coordinates: 45°56'20.1"N 80°54'15.6"W
Description: Cylindrical mast, white daymark
Location: French River
Directions: Accessible by boat
Opened: 1875
Automated: 1934
Deactivated: Active
Height: 12 feet (3.7 metres)
Focal Height: 22 feet (6.7 metres)
Signal: White flash every 4 seconds
Access: Grounds open, interior closed

Name: Giants Tomb Island
Coordinates: 44°52'49.3"N 80°00'28.3"W
Description: Skeleton Tower
Location: Giants Tomb Island
Directions: Accessible by boat
Opened: 1969
Automated: 1969
Deactivated: Active
Lens: Dioptric of the 7th order
Height: 48 feet (14.6 metres)
Focal Height: 56 feet (17.2 metres)
Signal: White flash every 4 seconds
Access: Closed

Name: Gravenhurst Narrows
Coordinates: 44°57'17.6"N 79°24'22.9"W
Description: White pyramid tower, red roof
Location: Gravenhurst
Directions: Accessible by boat
Opened: 1905
Automated: 1924
Deactivated: Active
Lens: Dioptric light of the sixth order
Height: 26 feet (8 metres)
Focal Height: 30 feet (9.1 metres)
Signal: Fixed red
Access: Grounds open, interior closed

Name: Jones Island Range Front
Coordinates: 45°18'55.5"N 80°16'57.0"W
Description: Square, pyramidal tower
Location: Jones Island
Directions: Accessible by boat
Opened: 1894
Deactivated: Active
Height: 36 feet (11.1 metres)
Focal Height: 41 feet (12.4 metres)
Signal: Fixed white
Access: Closed

Name: Jones Island Range Rear
Coordinates: 45°17'58.3"N 80°15'25.2"W
Description: Square, pyramidal tower
Location: Jones Island
Directions: Accessible by boat
Opened: 1894
Deactivated: Active
Height: 51 feet (15.5 metres)
Focal Height: 61 feet (18.7 metres)
Signal: Fixed white
Access: Closed

Name: Rosseau
Coordinates: 45°14'47.0"N 79°38'18.8"W
Description: White square tower, red upper
Location: Rosseau
Directions: From Rosseau, head southeast on ON-141 E and turn right onto Bright St where the lighthouse is seen
Opened: 1890
Automated: 1924
Deactivated: 2011
Lens: Dioptric
Height: 26 feet (8 metres)
Focal Height: 30 feet (9.1 metres)
Signal: White flash every 4 seconds
Access: Closed

Name: Southeast Bay
Coordinates: 46°11'48.4"N 79°25'19.7"W
Description: White square tower
Location: Lake Nippissing
Directions: From Callander, head northwest on ON-654 W for 4.5 km and turn right onto Lighthouse Rd where the lighthouse is 1.3 km
Opened: 1887
Automated: Ca. 1924
Deactivated: Active
Height: 29 feet (8.7 metres)
Focal Height: 31 feet (9.4 metres)
Signal: Sector shows red, white and green
Access: Closed

Name: Spruce Shoal
Coordinates: 45°19'54.3"N 80°15'30.2"W
Description: White octagonal tower
Location: Spruce Shoal
Directions: Accessible by boat
Opened: 1908
Automated: 1908
Deactivated: 1949
Height: 21 feet (6.4 metres)
Signal: Flashing white
Access: Closed

Name: Wilson Channel Range Front
Coordinates: 46°19'21.5"N 83°58'55.6"W
Description: White square structure
Location: Desbarats
Directions: See from Bernt Gilbertson Bridge/ON-548 N
Opened: 1905
Automated: 1947
Deactivated: Active
Lens: Dioptric of the 7th order
Height: 27 feet (8.3 metres)
Focal Height: 69 feet (20.9 metres)
Signal: Fixed red
Access: Closed

Name: Wilson Channel Range Rear
Coordinates: 46°19'26.0"N 83°58'47.4"W
Description: White square structure
Location: Desbarats
Directions: See from Bernt Gilbertson Bridge/ON-548 N
Opened: 1905
Automated: 1947
Deactivated: Active
Lens: Catoptric
Height: 26 feet (7.9 metres)
Focal Height: 117 feet (35.8 metres)
Signal: Fixed red
Access: Closed

Cape North Lighthouse, Eastern Ontario Region

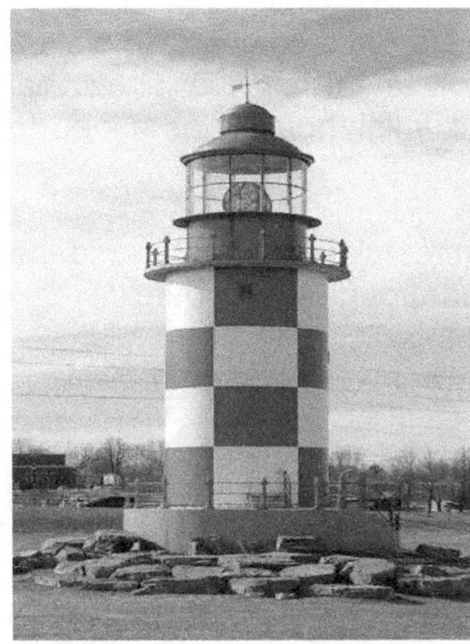

The Cape North Lighthouse began life as the Cape Race Lighthouse in Newfoundland where it opened in 1856. It was constructed of cast iron plates which were bolted together. When it was decided that a more powerful light was needed, the current Cape Race Lighthouse was built. The original Cape Race Lighthouse was moved to Cape North in Cape Breton, Nova Scotia in 1909 where it operated until 1980.

The National Museum of Science and Technology in Ottawa was looking for a lighthouse for their exhibit, and when plans to demolish the Cape North Lighthouse were announced, the Museum was able to acquire it.

The huge cast iron plates were shipped to Ottawa and the lighthouse was re-assembled at the Museum's Technology Park.

Description: Circular tower of cast iron plates

Location: Ottawa

Directions: Corner of Lancaster and Russell Rd, Ottawa

Coordinates: 45°24'07.4"N 75°37'25.7"W

Opened: 1980

Automated: 1980

Lens: Third-order Fresnel

Height: 95 feet (29 metres)

Focal Height: 112 feet (34 metres)

Visitor Access: Grounds open, tower open in museum hours

Cobourg East Pierhead Lighthouse, Eastern Ontario Region

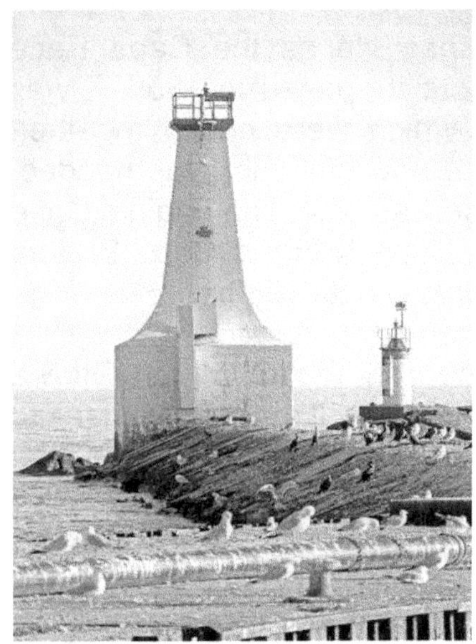

In 1829, a group of businessmen started a company to build a harbour in Cobourg. After involvement by the Provincial Government, piers were built and a lighthouse was added to the east pier in 1844.

The harbour helped stimulate commercial interests, as did the completion of a railway from Peterborough to Cobourg.

The present pyramidal concrete tower was opened in 1924.

Description: White pyramidal tower, red upper portion

Location: Cobourg

Directions: Tip of the eastern breakwater in Cobourg

Coordinates: 43°57'09.4"N 78°09'52.6"W

Opened: 1924

Automated: 1981

Deactivated: Active

Height: 40 feet (12.2 metres)

Focal Height: 49 feet (15 metres)

Signal: Red flash every two seconds

Foghorn Signal: Two 4 second blasts per minute

Visitor Access: Grounds open, interior closed

De Watteville Island Range Lighthouse, Eastern Ontario Region

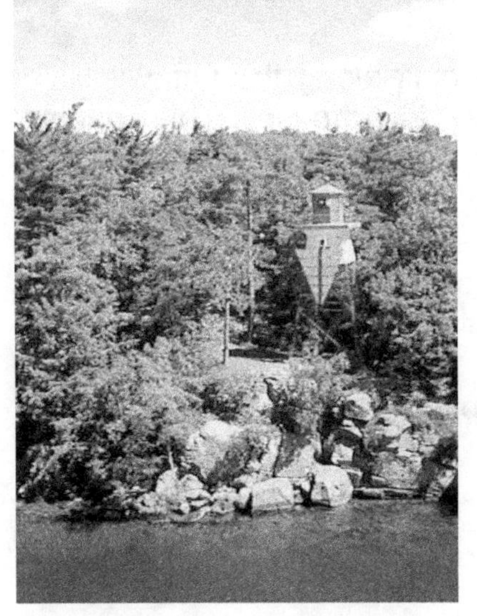

In 1927, range lights were built on De Watteville Island and on the mainland to the northeast. The Front range on the island, was 30 feet high. The rear range on the mainland had a focal height of 69 feet. Both signals were fixed white.

In 1969, the front range light was replaced by a white circular concrete tower with a red top. The skeleton rear tower has a triangular orange daymark with a vertical black stripe.

De Watteville Island Range Front

Description: White cylindrical tower,

Location: De Watteville Island

Directions: Accessible by boat

Coordinates: 44°32'56.4"N 75°44'00.2"W

Opened: 1960

Automated: 1960

Deactivated: Active

Height: 22 feet (6.7 metres)

Focal Height: 27 feet (8.2 metres)

Signal: Fixed white

Visitor Access: Closed

De Watteville Island Range Rear

Description: Red skeleton tower

Location: Mainland

Directions: 451 Hillcrest Rd, Brockville

Coordinates: 44°33'00.5"N75°43'51.9"W

Opened: 1927

Automated: 1937

Deactivated: Active

Height: 48 feet (14.5 metres)

Focal Height: 69 feet (21 metres)

Signal: Fixed white

Visitor Access: Closed

Deep River Islet Lighthouse, Eastern Ontario Region

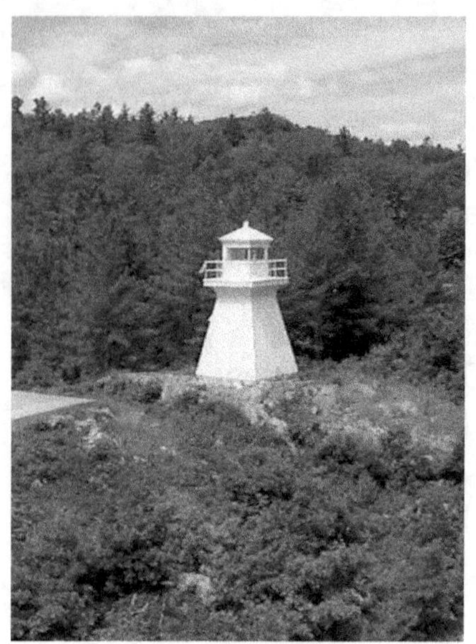

In 1873, three lighthouses were built along the Ottawa River including the Deep River Islet Lighthouse. This original lighthouse was a square wooden building of 22 feet.

The Ottawa River becomes constricted at this point with the Deep River Islet on the Ontario side and a long peninsula on the Quebec side.

In 1913, a new lighthouse replaced it, with a sixth-order Fresnel lens.

Description: White square tapered tower

Location: Deep River Islet

Directions: Accessible by boat

Coordinates: 46°00'45.9"N 77°16'49.6"W

Opened: 1913

Automated: 1924

Deactivated: Active

Lens: Sixth-order Fresnel

Height: 29 feet (9 metres)

Focal Height: 52 feet (15.8 metres)

Signal: White flash every 4 seconds

Visitor Access: Closed

Dickinson Landing Lighthouse, Eastern Region

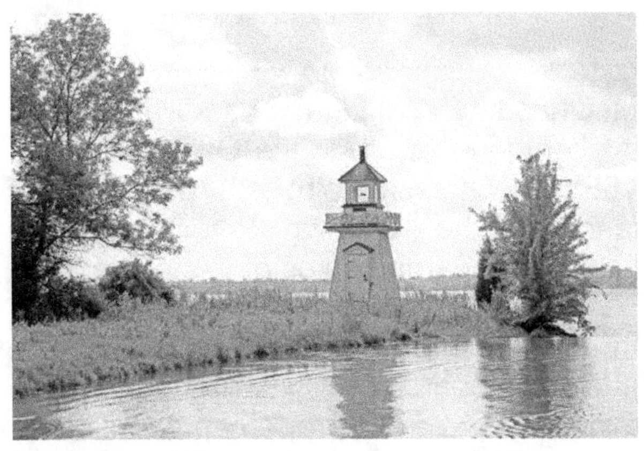

After completion of the Rideau Canal in 1932, the town of Brockville requested that the Cornwall Canal be constructed in fears that St. Lawrence River traffic would bypass the town. Plans were for the Canal to run from the St Lawrence River from Cornwall to Dickson Landing, some 16 kilometres away. While work began in 1834, the canal was not completed until 1843 due to a financial depression and the Upper Canada Rebellion of 1837.

In 1865, the Cornwall Canal Lighthouse was built to mark the upper entrance to the Cornwall Canal. By 1891, this lighthouse was in poor shape and was replaced, with the new station know as the Dickinson Landing Lighthouse. In the 1950s, the St. Lawrence Seaway was being built which resulted in flooding of many villages including Dickinson Landing. At that time the Lighthouse was moved to the Upper Canada Village.

Description: Square tapering wooden tower

Location: Upper Canada Village

Directions: 13740 County Rd 2, Morrisburg

Coordinates: 44°56'39.8"N 75°03'59.4"W

Opened: 1891

Automated: 1910

Deactivated: 1950s

Lens: Dioptric

Height: 22 feet (6.7 metres)

Focal height: 22 feet (6.4 metres)

Signal: Fixed white

Visitor Access: Grounds open, interior closed

McQuestin Point Lighthouse, Eastern Ontario Region

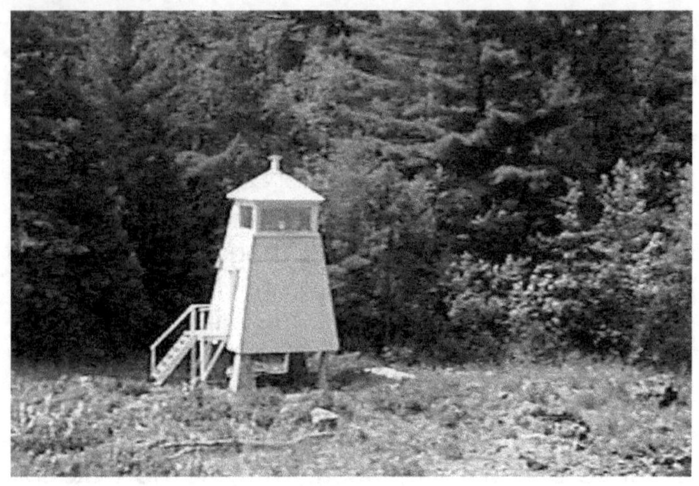

McQuestin Point Lighthouse was one of six lighthouse built on the Ottawa River in 1883. McQuestin Point is a peninsula of land in the Ottawa River and the lighthouse warned ships of this obstacle.

In 1944, the Chalk River Laboratories, a nuclear research facility was opened and this nuclear reactor property prevents land access to the lighthouse. It is therefore best seen from the river by boat.

Description: White square structure

Location: Deep River

Directions: Accessible by boat

Coordinates: 46°03'52.6"N 77°22'52.3"W

Opened: 1921

Automated: 1924

Deactivated: Active

Lens: Dioptric seventh-order

Height: 31 feet (6.5 metres)

Focal Height: 26 feet (10 metres)

Signal: White flash every 4 seconds

Visitor Access: Grounds open, interior closed

Point Petre Lighthouse, Eastern Ontario Region

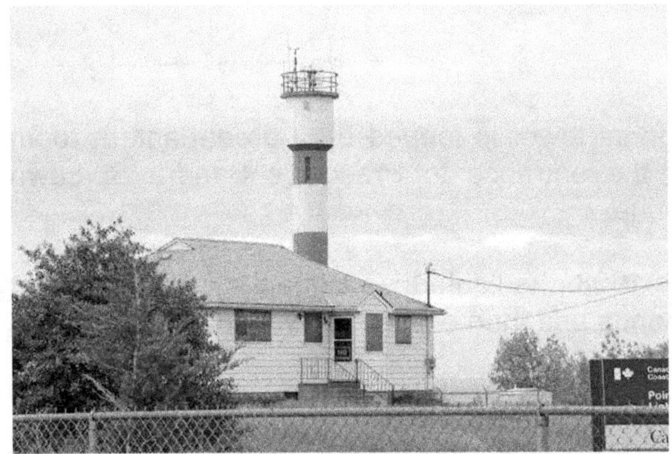

The present tower was erected in 1967, replacing the original 1833 tower. While the local Historical Society was in negotiations to take over the old tower, the government demolished it.

Description: White cylindrical tower, red horizontal bands

Location: South tip of the Quinte Peninsula

Directions: From South Bay, head southwest on County Rd 13 for 2.0 km and turn left onto County Rd 10. After 1.5 km, turn left onto Royal Rd and continue for 7.4 km. Turn left onto County Rd 24/Regional Rd 24 and after 3.2 km, continue onto Point Petre Rd where you will see the lighthouse

Coordinates: 43°50'25.1"N 77°09'07.2"W

Opened: 1832

Automated: 1974

Deactivated: Active

Lens: Reflector

Height: 63 feet (19.3 metres)

Focal Height: 71 feet (21.7 metres)

Signal: Half-second-flash, one-second eclipse, half-second flash, five-and-a-half-second eclipse.

Foghorn Signal: 3 second blast every 30 seconds

Visitor Access: Closed

Prescott Heritage Harbour Lighthouse, Eastern Ontario Region

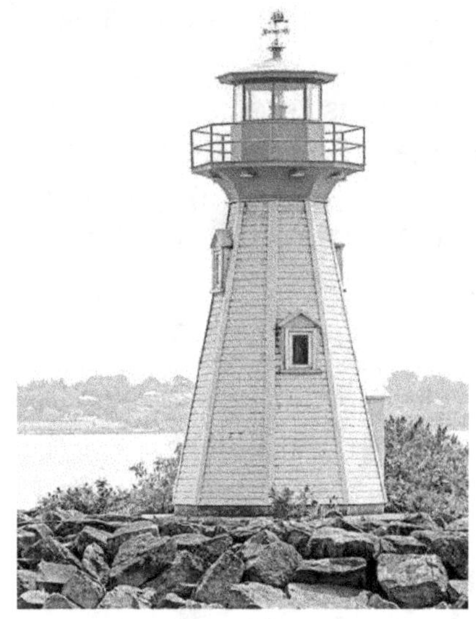

This white octagonal tower is topped by a green lantern room and situated at the entrance to Prescott's Sandra S. Lawn Harbour and Marina.

It was built in the 1908. the lighthouse signals a green light that is on for two seconds and then eclipse for two seconds.

Description: White octagonal tower, green upper portion

Location: Prescott

Directions: 191 Water St E, Prescott (End of pier)

Coordinates: 44°42'35.0"N 75°30'34.4"W

Opened: 1908

Deactivated: Active

Lens: Fresnel

Height: 22 feet (6.8 metres)

Focal Height: 27 feet (8.3 metres)

Signal: Green flash for two seconds, eclipse two seconds

Visitor Access: Closed

Prescott Lighthouse, Eastern Ontario Region

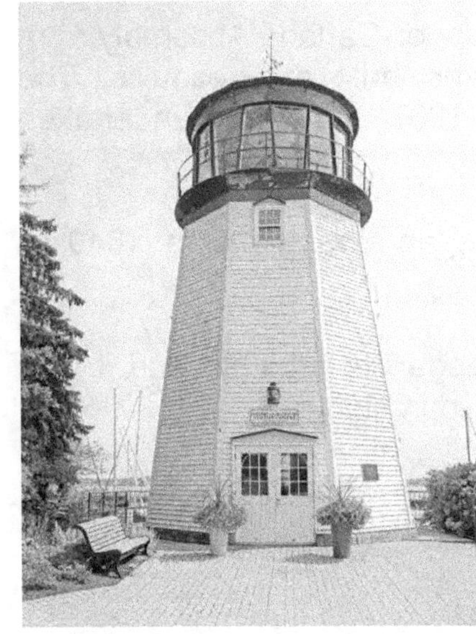

This lighthouse serves as a welcome center for the City of Prescott. On the lower level is a a gift shop and ice cream stand. The lighthouse has a Fresnel lens donated by the Canadian Coast Guard. During the summer, visitors could climb to the top for a great view. However, this seems to have discontinued.

Description: White octagonal wooden tower

Location: Prescott

Directions: 181 Water St E, Prescott

Coordinates: 44°42'36.4"N 75°30'42.1"W

Opened: 1989

Lens: Fifth order Fresnel

Height: 40 feet (12 metres)

Visitor Access: Grounds and interior open in summer season

Presqu'ile Point Lighthouse, Eastern Ontario Region

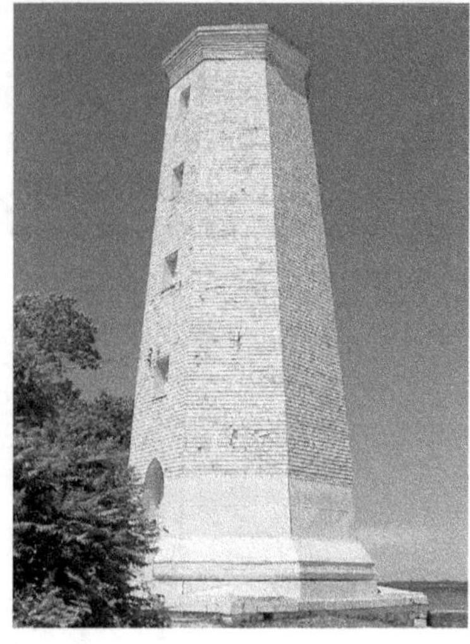

In 1835, a request was sent to the Upper Canada Assembly from area citizens, for a lighthouse to be built at Presqu'ile. The government approved a contract in 1837 and it was undertaken by John McLeod who completed it.

The Presqu'Ile Point Lighthouse began operations in 1840. A foghorn was added in 1907.

By 1894 the Lighthouse's exterior began to crumble and it was sheathed in a wood frame and covered in shingles.

The top cupola was removed in 1965 when the station was deactivated.

Description: White octagonal tower, red upper portion

Location: Presqu'ile Provincial Park (Admission charge)

Directions: From Brighton. head southwest on Ontario St/ Reg. Rd. 66 for 2.7 km, make a slight right on Presqu'Ile Pkwy and continue 4. 0 km. Continue onto Lighthouse Ln/Presqu'Ile Pkwy for 4.3 km where you find the lighthouse.

Coordinates: 43°59'52.1"N 77°40'38.3"W

Opened: 1840

Automated: 1935

Deactivated: 1965

Lens: Reflectors

Height: 68 feet (20.7 metres)

Focal Height: 77 feet (23.5 metres)

Signal: Fixed red

Foghorn Signal: Six second blast every minute

Visitor Access: Grounds open, interior closed

Windmill Point Lighthouse, Eastern Ontario Region

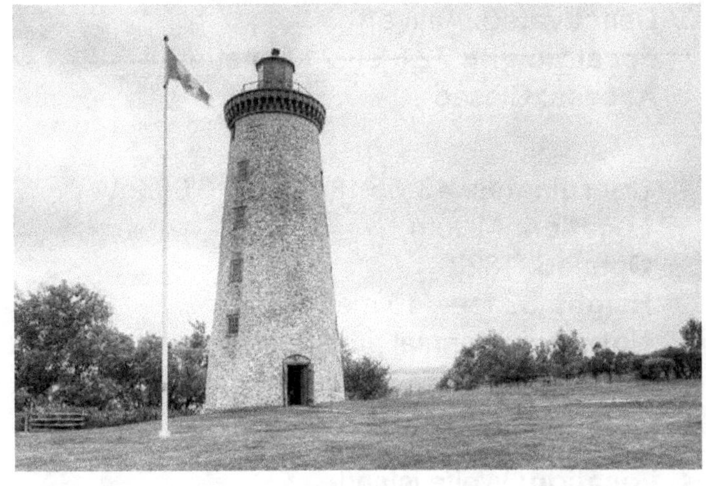

This structure has led an interesting life. It was built Ca.1830 as a windmill and served the local community by milling grain.

In 1838 it became part of the Upper Canada Rebellion. Rebels had fled to the U.S. after an armed march on Toronto in late 1837. About 250 rebels invaded Upper Canada at Prescott, expecting the local people to join them. They held a position at the Windmill. They were soon surrounded by far superior numbers and were forced to surrender after a few days.

In 1873, the Department of Marine purchased the windmill and converted it to a lighthouse. The lighthouse was active until 1978. It was listed as a Heritage Lighthouse on December 20, 2013.

Description: Circular stone tower

Location: Prescott

Directions: From Prescott, head east on County Rd 2 for 1.5 km and turn right onto Windmill Rd where you will find the lighthouse

Coordinates: 44°43'15.3"N 75°29'13.7"W

Opened: 1873

Automated: 1928

Deactivated: 1978

Lens: Catoptric

Height: 62 feet (18.9 metres)

Signal: Fixed white

Visitor Access: Grounds open, interior open in season

Name: False Ducks
Description: Hexagonal, reinforced-concrete
Directions: Swetman Island
Automated: 1965
Height: 62 feet (19 metres)
Signal: Red flash every 4 seconds
Coordinates: 43°55'18.8"N 77°03'08.9"W
Location: Swetman Island
Opened: 1965
Deactivated: Active
Focal Height: 72 feet (21.8 metres)
Access: Closed

Name: False Ducks (1967)
Description: Circular stone tower
Directions: 2065 County Rd 13, Milford
Lens: Third-order Fresnel
Access: Grounds open, interior closed
Coordinates: 43°55'18.8"N 77°3'08.9"W
Location: Milford
Opened: 1828
Height: 33 feet (10 metres)
Note: A centennial project

Name: Knapp Point
Description: White tower
Directions: Accessible by ferry
Automated: 1947
Lens: Catoptric
Focal Height: 37 feet (11.3 metres)
Access: Closed
Coordinates: 44°13'56.4"N 76°3'51.9"W
Location: Wolfe island
Opened: 1874
Deactivated: 2000
Height: 21 feet (6.4 metres)
Signal: White flash every 4 seconds

Name: L'Orignal Range Front
Description: White square wooden tower
Directions: 110 Des Chalets St, L'Orignal
Automated: 1924
Lens: Sixth-order Fresnel
Focal Height: 57 feet (17.3 metres)
Access: Closed
Coordinates: 45°37'32.6"N 74°2'14.8"W
Location: L'Orignal
Opened: 1915
Deactivated: 1990s
Height: 29 feet (8.8 metres)
Signal: Fixed white

Name: L'Orignal Range Rear
Description: White square wooden tower
Directions: Chem. Larochelle, L'Orignal
Automated: 1924
Lens: Sixth-order Fresnel
Focal Height: 60 feet (18.2 metres)
Access: Closed
Coordinates: 45°37'31.8"N 74°2'18.2"W
Location: L'Orignal
Opened: 1915
Deactivated: 1990s
Height: 33 feet (10 metres)
Signal: Fixed white

Name: Lancaster Range
Description: White hexagonal tower, red top
Directions: Accessible by boat
Automated: 1925
Lens: Dioptric
Focal Height: 33 feet (10 metres)
Access: Closed
Coordinates: 45°06'01.2"N 74°29'28.7"W
Location: Lancaster Bar
Opened: 1885
Deactivated: Active
Height: 30 feet (9.1 metres)
Signal: Fixed white

Name: Main Duck Island
Description: Octagonal concrete tower
Directions: Accessible by boat
Automated: 1978
Lens: Third order Fresnel
Focal Height: 77 feet (23.7 m)
Foghorn Signal: 2 blasts every 45 seconds
Coordinates: 43°55'52.1"N 76°38'18.4"W
Location: Main Duck Island
Opened: 1914
Deactivated: Active
Height: 81 feet (24.8 m)
Signal: White flash every six seconds
Access: Grounds open, interior closed

Name: Morris Island
Description: Square wooden tower
Directions: Accessible by boat
Automated: 1924
Lens: Catoptric
Focal Height: 29 feet (8.8 metres)
Access: Closed (Private)
Coordinates: 45°27'30.7"N 76°16'59.5"W
Location: Morris Island
Opened: 1873
Deactivated: 1983
Height: 29 feet 8.8 metres)
Signal: Fixed white

Name: Nine Mile Point
Description: White cylindrical tower
Directions: Western tip of Simcoe Island
Automated: 1988
Lens: Fourth-order Fresnel
Focal Height: 53 feet (16.1 metres)
Access: Closed
Coordinates: 44°09'05.5"N 76°33'20.7"W
Location: Simcoe Island
Opened: 1834
Deactivated: Active
Height: 48 feet (14.6 metres)
Signal: 2 second white flash, 8 second eclipse

Name: Pigeon Island
Description: White square skeleton tower
Directions: Accessible by boat
Automated: 1937
Lens: Fourth-order Fresnel
Focal Height: 69 feet (21.1 metres)
Access: Closed
Coordinates: 44°03'59.4"N 76°32'59.3"W
Location: Pigeon Island
Opened: 1908
Deactivated: Active
Height: 67 feet (20.4 metres)
Signal: White flash every 4 seconds

Name: Prince Edward Point
Coordinates: 43°56'14.2"N 76°51'32.0"W
Description: White skeleton tower
Location: Milford
Directions: From South Bay, head northeast on County Rd 13 for 10.7 km and continue onto Long Point Rd. After 7.2 km continue straight onto Traverse Ln where the lighthouse is 1.2 km
Opened: 1881
Automated: 1941
Deactivated: Active
Lens: Fourth-order Fresnel
Height: 43 feet (13 metres)
Focal Height: 48 feet (14.4 metres)
Signal: Flashing white every 5 seconds
Access: Grounds open, interior closed

Name: Salmon Point
Coordinates: 43°51'25.4"N 77°14'39.4"W
Description: Square wooden tower
Location: Milford
Directions: From the Village of Salmon Point, head south on Point Rd/Salmon Point Rd for 4.6 km to find the lighthouse
Opened: 1871
Deactivated: 1913
Lens: Fourth-order Fresnel
Height: 29 feet (8.8 metres)
Focal Height: 35 feet (10.6 metres)
Access: Closed

Name: Sand Point
Coordinates: 45°29'19.7"N 76°26'04.2"W
Description: White square structure
Location: Sand Point
Directions: From County Rd1 at Sand Point, head northeast on Wharf Rd and the lighthouse is a short distance
Opened: 1909
Automated: 1924
Deactivated: Active
Lens: Seventh-order Fresnel
Height: 22 feet (6.7 metres)
Focal Height: 23 feet (7 metres)
Signal: Flashing white
Access: Grounds open, interior closed

Name: Scotch Bonnet Island
Coordinates: 43°53'58.2"N 77°32'32.8"W
Description: Triangular skeleton tower
Location: Scotch Bonnet Island
Directions: Accessible by boat
Opened: 1969
Automated: 1963
Deactivated: Active
Lens: Fourth-order Fresnel
Height: 54 feet (16.4 metres)
Signal: 1 second flash, 3 second eclipse
Access: Closed

Name: Wolfe Island
Coordinates: 44°14'19.9"N 76°11'02.8"W
Description: White tower
Location: Wolfe Island
Directions: Accessible by boat
Opened: 1911
Automated: 1954
Deactivated: Active
Lens: Catoptric
Height: 21 feet (6.4 metres)
Focal Height: 37 feet (11.3 metres)
Signal: White flash every 4 seconds
Access: Closed

Burlington Canal Lighthouses, Golden Horseshoe Region

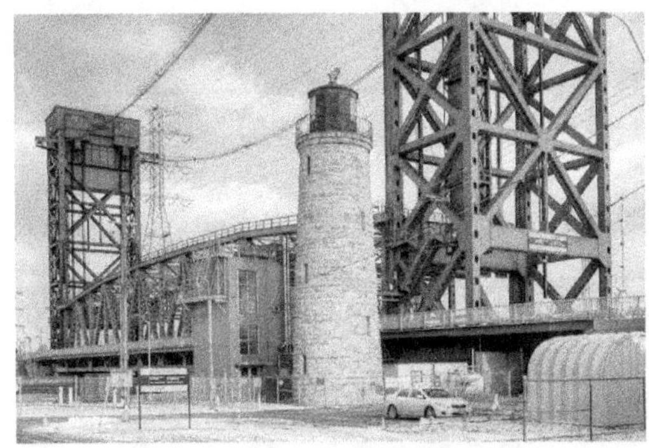

In 1824 the Upper Canada Assembly authorized a canal to be built to provide a harbour at the head of Lake Ontario. The Upper Canada Assembly authorized a canal be built to connect Lake Ontario and Burlington Bay (Renamed Hamilton Harbour in 1919). An £8,500 contract was awarded to an American Firm of Strowbridge, Hayes, and McKeen with a completion date of October 1, 1825.

The contractors ran into trouble from the beginning. The ground was very compacted and difficult to drive piles, storms interrupted and flooded the excavation, and dredging equipment was delayed. Before the coming of steam powered dredging, the work at Burlington Canal involved fifty workers in hand labour in difficult and dangerous conditions. The completion date was extended for 1 year which passed without fulfillment. In 1826 there was an official opening ceremony although only small ships could be accommodated. By 1827 the contractor and the government were at odds and in January 1828 fierce storms left the breakwater and piers in ruins. It was not until 1930 before larger ships could use the canal.

In 1837 John Williams was contracted to build a 50 foot wood lighthouse at the canal. In 1856 a passing steamship caused a fire to spread on the pier, which destroyed the lighthouse. John Brown, who built the Imperial Towers, completed the building of Burlington Canal Main Lighthouse in 1857. It is composed of large blocks of dolomite. It received a fourth-order Fresnel lens in 1911 and was electrified in 1922.

In 1845 a 14 foot high Front Range lighthouse was built. In 1905 a steel tower replaced it and in 1910 it was again replaced, this time by a forty-one foot steel tower. The current white, square base concrete tower was built in 1939.

Burlington Canal Main Lighthouse was listed as as a Heritage Lighthouse in 2021.

	Canal Main	**Canal Pier**
Location:	Burlington	Burlington
Coordinates:	43°17'54.5"N 79°47'42.8"W	43°18'03.6"N 79°47'26.1"W
Opened:	1857	1939
Automated:	N/A	N/a
Deactivated:	1961	1961

Lens:	Fourth-order Fresnel	
Height:	23 feet (7 metres)	43 feet (13.1 metres)
Focal Height:	32 feet (9.7 metres)	48 feet (14.5 metres)
Signal:	Flashing red every 4 seconds	Fixed red
Visitor Access:	Grounds open, interior closed	

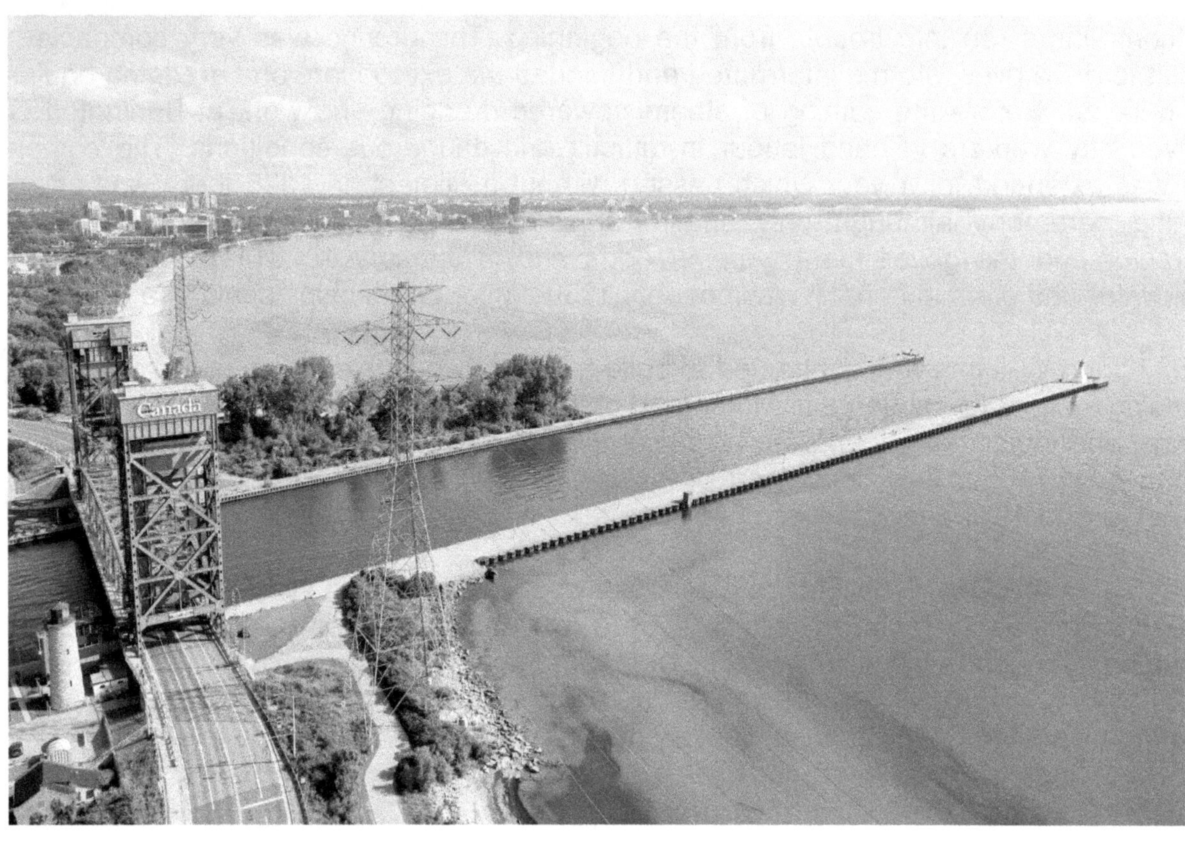

The Canal Pier at end of pier and Canal Main at bottom left

Gibraltar Point Lighthouse, Golden Horseshoe Region

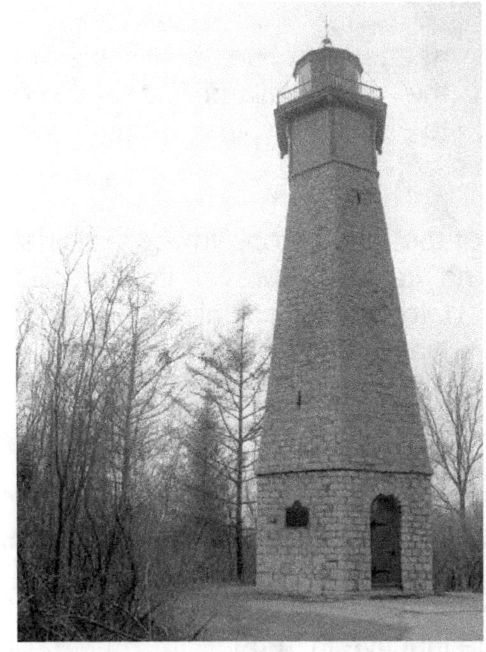

Before 1793, the capital of Upper Canada was Niagara-on-the-Lake and tensions were high with the provinces U.S. neighbours. It was decided to move the capital to Toronto, then known as York. Fort York was built as well as defence positions on Centre Island in the harbour. As protection for the harbour, Gibraltar Point Lighthouse was built at the southern point of Centre Island. It is the oldest surviving lighthouse on the Great Lakes

The lighthouse is a six-sided structure composed of limestone from a quarry near Niagara Falls. It originally was fifty-two feet high (sixteen metres) but an additional thirty-two feet (nine metres) was added. The lighting system was upgraded in 1878 and 1883, and in 1915 a fourth-order Fresnel lens was installed. At that time the signal was changed to a white light every four seconds. In 1945 it was changed again to a fixed green light.

The lighthouse was automated in 1918 and decommissioned in 1959. It is said to be haunted by John Paul Radelmuller, the first Keeper. He was apparently murdered on the 2nd of January, 1815. The culprits were thought to be soldiers who had argued with him.

Location: Toronto Islands

Directions: From the Jack Layton Ferry Terminal at 11 Queens Quay W, Toronto, take the Centre Island Ferry and take the footpath southwest to the other side of the island.

Coordinates: 43.613667°N 79.385278°W

Opened: 1808

Automated: 1918

Deactivated: 1959

Lens: Fourth-order Fresnel

Height: 84 feet (25 metres)

Signal: Fixed green light

Visitor Access: The exterior is available to visit but the lighthouse interior is closed.

Mohawk Island Lighthouse, Golden Horseshoe Region

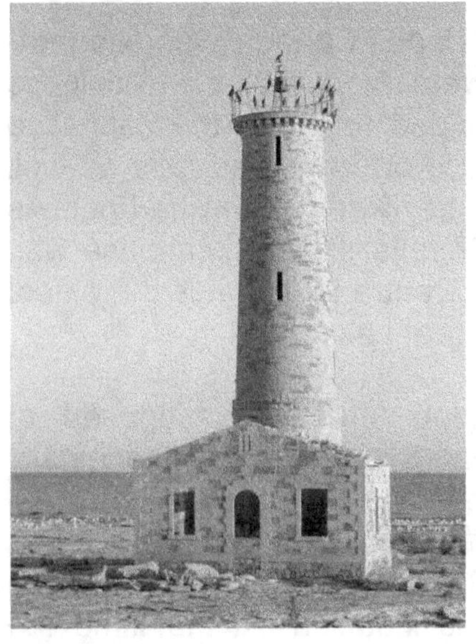

Mohawk Island Lighthouse needed to be built due to construction on portions of the 1st Welland Canal. The lighthouse was constructed to protect ships around the southern end of the canal.

The structure is now a ruin but the intact stone tower remains. It is often visited by boat and kayak. However it is closed between April 1 and August 31 to protect colonies of nesting birds. It has been designated a National Wildlife Area.

The lighthouse has been witness to tragedy during it's life. In December of 1932 the last Keeper, Richard Foster and his son set off for shore by boat after closing the station. They never arrived alive but it was several days before the bodies were found near shore. Autopsies showed they had died of hypothermia rather than drowning. This event seems to have triggered automation of the station, It was subsequently made inactive in 1969.

Description: Conical limestone tower

Location: Dunnville

Directions: Boat required. There is a long view of the Lighthouse from Rock Point Provincial Park (42°50'29.8"N 79°32'36.0"W)

Coordinates: 42.834055°N 79.522820°W

Opened: 1838

Automated: 1933

Deactivated: 1969

Lens: Ten lamps, each set in a parabolic reflector

Height: 59 feet (18 metres)

Signal: White light, flash, six-second eclipse, flash, eighteen-second eclipse

Visitor Access: The island is now Mohawk Island National Wildlife Area. Public access to the island is prohibited during nesting season of the birds, which runs from April 1 to July 31.

Niagara River Range Lighthouses, Golden Horseshoe Region

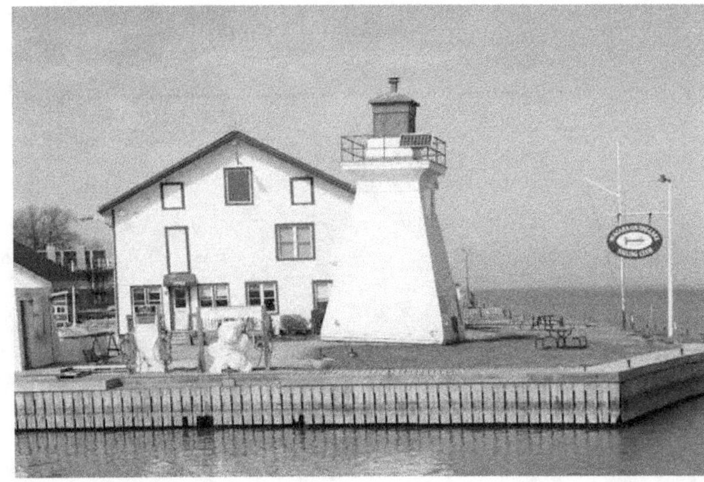

Front range Image

In 1804, the Mississauga Point Lighthouse was built to mark the entrance to the Niagara River. It was the first lighthouse on the Great Lakes. It was damaged in 1913 in the war with the United States and was removed in 1814 to build Fort Mississauga.

In 1904, the government built the two range Lighthouses. A fog alarm was installed at this time as well, which began operations in 1905.

Niagara River Range Front

Description: White tower, red upper

Location: Niagara-on-the-Lake

Directions: 2 Melville St, Niagara-on-the-Lake

Coordinates: 43°15'19.7"N 79°03'42.4"W

Opened: 1904

Automated: 1937

Deactivated: Active

Lens: Long focus reflectors

Height: 34 feet (10.4 metres)

Focal Height: 45 feet (13.8 metres)

Signal: Fixed Red

Niagara River Range Rear

Description: White tower, red upper

Location: Niagara-on-the-Lake

Directions: 247 Ricardo St, Niagara-on-the-Lake

Coordinates: 43°15'13.7"N 79°03'37.6"W

Opened: 1904

Automated: 1937

Deactivated: Active

Lens: Long focus reflectors

Height: 45 feet (13.8 metres)

Focal Height: 50 feet (14.3 metres)

Signal: Fixed Red

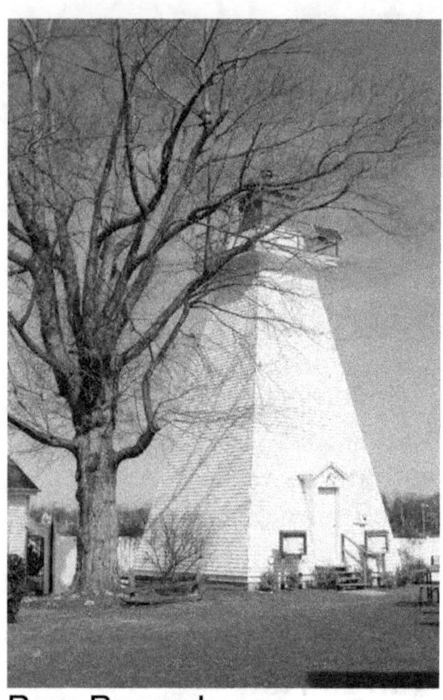
Rear Range Image

Foghorn Signal: Five-second blast every two minutes

Visitor Access: Closed

Visitor Access: Closed

Oakville Lighthouse, Golden Horseshoe Region

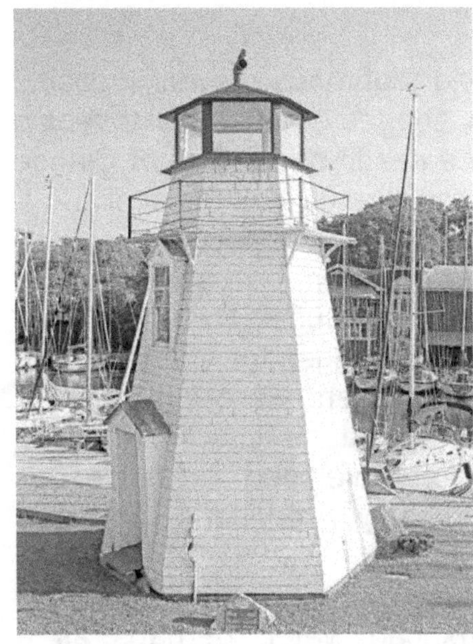

The first lighthouse at the Oakville harbour was a wooden octagonal tower which opened in 1838. It was destroyed by a storm in 1886.

A new lighthouse was opened in 1888. It is a hexagonal wooden tower. This structure was moved three times in the next three years due to damage to the pier.

After the lighthouse was deactivated in 1960, it was moved to the Oakville Yacht club.

Description: Hexagonal wooden tower

Location: Oakville

Directions: 97 Forsythe St, Oakville

Coordinates: 43°26'30.3"N 79°40'10.0"W

Opened: 1888

Automated: 1940

Deactivated: 1960

Lens: Sixth-order Fresnel

Height: 31 feet (9.4 metres)

Focal Height: 39 feet (11.9 metres)

Signal: Fixed white

Visitor Access: Grounds open, interior closed

Point Abino, Lighthouse, Golden Hoseshoe Region

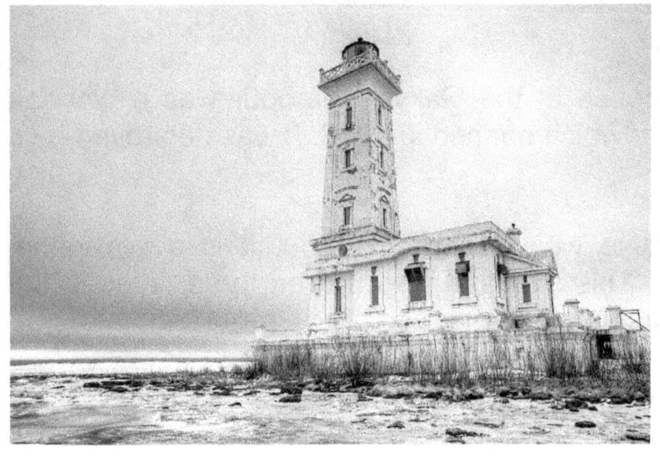

The Point Albino Lighthouse is an imposing structure. It is suggested that Point Albino was named for a Jesuit priest, Father Claude Aveneau which apparently sounds similar.

Point Albino juts out from the eastern end of Lake Erie across from Buffalo, New York and presents a serious danger for ships. By the late 1890's, ship owners were calling for a lighthouse at the tip. At the time, Point Albino had recently been developed for residences for the rich, primarily Americans, and was and is, a gated community.

By 1907, ship masters were calling for a lightship in American water, perhaps as a compromise with the Point Albino residents. U.S. Congress passed a bill to fund a lightship and authorized $75,000 for its construction. By 1912, a lightship was completed and called Lightship LV 82. It had a steel hull and measured ninety-five feet long.

However in November of 1913, the Great Storm of 1913 hit the Great Lakes with hurricane force winds. Estimates were that waves often exceeded 35 ft (11 m). It was the worst storm recorded on the Great Lakes in its history, with nineteen ships sinking and more than two hundred and fifty crewmen lost. Included in this number was the Lightship LV 82 and all of its crew. In 1914, a diver found the remains in over sixty feet of water and two miles from it's station.

In 1915 the Department of Marine and Fisheries started planning for a Lighthouse to be built at Point Albino. By October of 1917, the lighthouse was open for service. The building was equipped with a third-order Fresnel lens as well as a fog alarm. It was overseen by head keepers, with the last, Lewis W. Anderson, present until 1989. At that time the station was automated and in 1995 the station was decommissioned. An extensive structural and exterior restoration took place in 2011.

Tours are conducted twice a month from May to October. The lighthouse was listed a National Historic Site of Canada in 1998.

Location: Fort Erie

Directions: In Port Colborne, head east on Killaly St E toward Fares St for 5.4 km and turn right onto Holloway Bay Rd N. After 1 km turn left onto Sherkston Rd and in another 4.8 km, turn right onto Point Abino Rd N. In 4.8 km you will see the lighthouse

Coordinates: 42.8361°N 79.0952°W

Opened: 1917

Automated: 1989

Deactivated: 1995

Lens: Third-order Fresnel

Height: 90 feet (28 metres)

Focal Height: 87 feet (27 metres)

Signal: Two seconds flash followed by two seconds eclipse

Foghorn Signal: triple blast each minute

Visitor Access: Tours are conducted twice a month from May to October

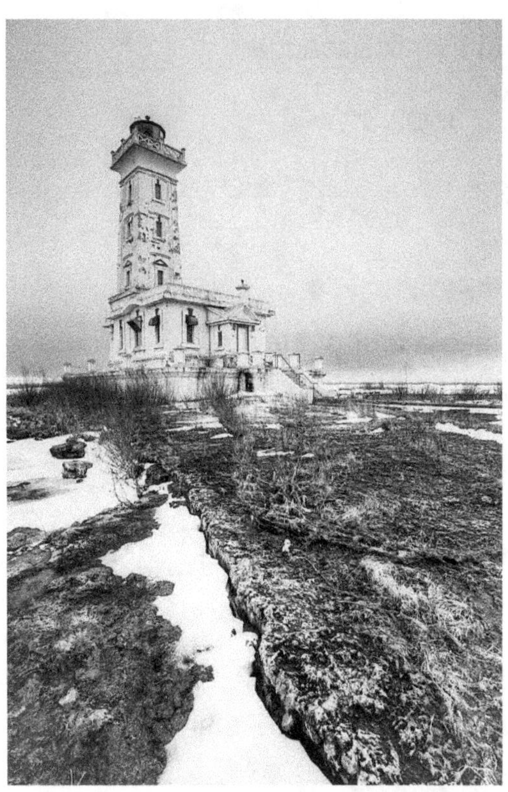

Port Credit Lighthouse, Golden Horseshoe Region

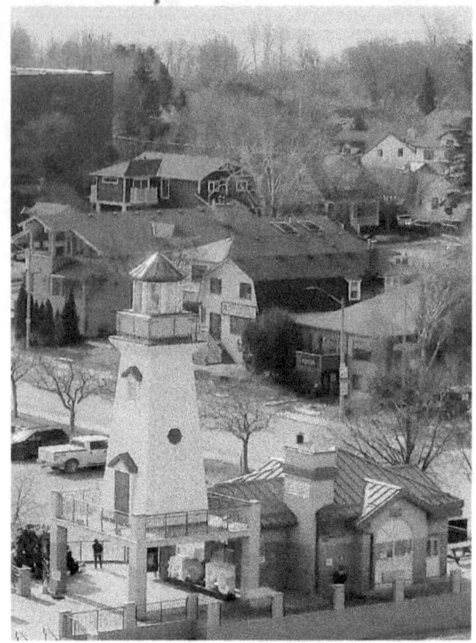

The first thing to note about this building is that it is a replica of a lighthouse that burned in 1936. That original structure opened in 1883. It had been deactivated in 1918 after the Credit River became unsuitable as a harbour. The lighthouse stood abandoned until it was destroyed by fire in 1936.

The Credit Valley Lions Club promoted the building of a replica of the original and it opened in a October 27, 1991 ceremony. It is active as a functioning lighthouse

Location: Mississauga

Directions: 105 Lakeshore Rd W, Mississauga

Coordinates: 43°33'01.3"N 79°35'09.8"W

Opened: 1991 (Original 1883)

Deactivated: (Original 1918)

Visitor Access: Visitors can take a tour of the structure. There is no charge for admission.

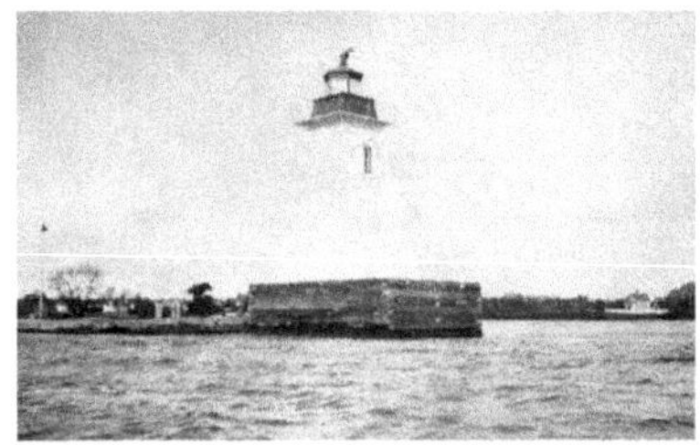

The original Lighthouse (Courtesy Library and Archives Canada)

Port Dalhousie Range Lighthouses, Golden Horseshoe Region

Rear Range

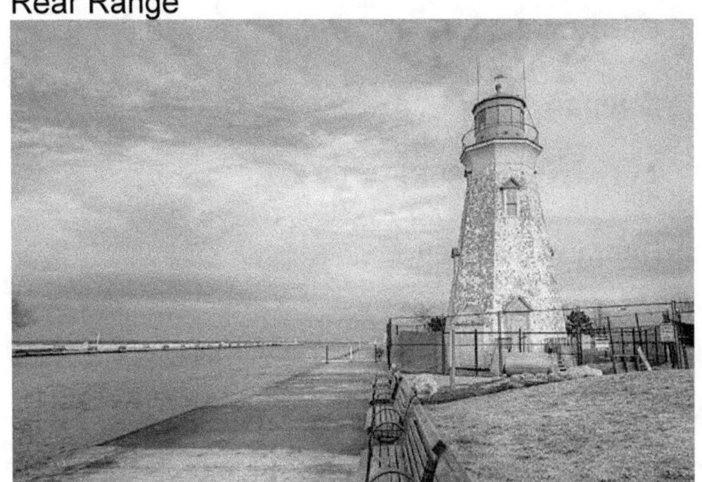

Throughout the life of the first three Welland Canals, lighthouses have been helping ship captains to safely enter the northern terminus at Port Dalhousie. The first lighthouse at Port Dalhousie, built in 1833, was destroyed in a heavy gale in 1837. The second lighthouse, opened in 1893 had a short life as well, as in 1898 it was struck by lightning and destroyed by fire. The present rear lighthouse was completed the same year and it has endured for over 125 years. It was moved from the pier to the shore as it was felt to be a safer site, as well as providing an better range from the Range Front Lighthouse.

In 1902 both Range lighthouses were electrified, and in 1908, a diaphone fog alarm was added. In 1912, the foghorn was modified to run on an oil engine.

Both Range Light where automated in 1968. The Rear Range light was deactivated in 1988, while the Front Range continued to operate. The building was rehabilitated in 2002 and in 2010. It was listed as a Recognized Federal Heritage Building in 1989.

Port Dalhousie Rear

Description: Octagonal wooden

Location: Port Dalhousie

Port Dalhousie Front

Description: Square wooden tower

Location: Port Dalhousie

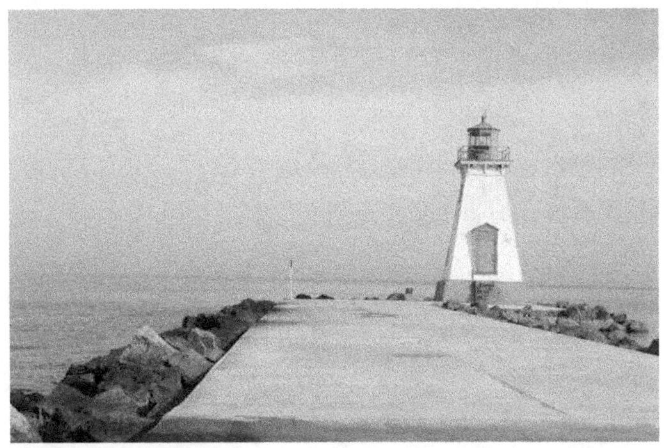

Front range

Directions: 57-61 Lighthouse Rd, St. Catharines

Coordinates: 43°12'25.2"N 79°15'44.0"W	**Coordinates:** 43°12'39.9"N 79°15'48.6"W
Opened: 1898	**Opened**: 1893
Automated: 1940	**Automated**: 1968
Deactivated: 1988	**Deactivated**: Active
Height: 46 feet (14 metres)	**Height:** 42 feet (13 metres)
Focal Height: 52 metres (16 feet)	**Focal Height**: 44 feet (13.3 metres)
Signal: Occulting white	**Signal**: Flash Green every 4 seconds
Visitor Access: Grounds open, tower closed	**Visitor Access:** Grounds open, tower closed

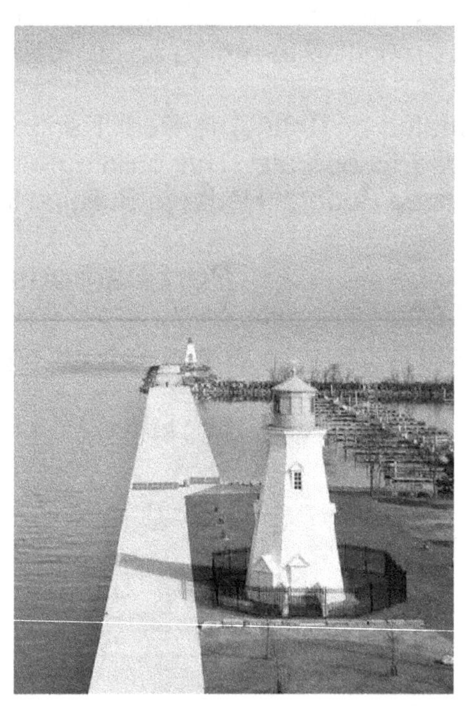

Port Weller Lighthouse, Golden Horseshoe Region

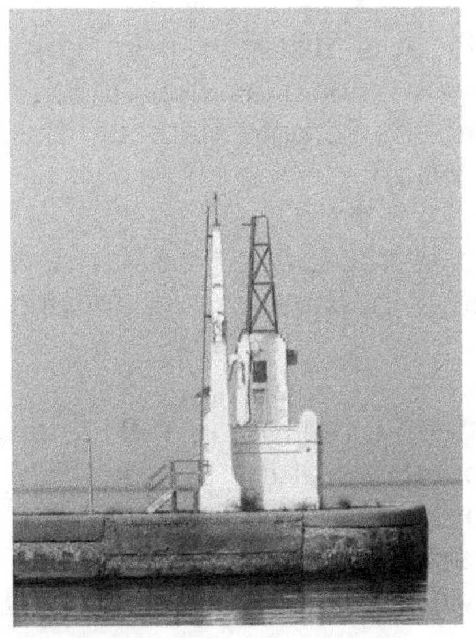

The current version of the Welland Canal is the fourth one, when the Lake Ontario entrance was moved to Port Weller. In 1931, the Port Weller Lighthouse was opened to guide ships to this entrance. A fog signal was included as well.

In 1936, a sixth-order dioptric upgrade was made to the lighthouse.

This Keepers dwelling and foghorn buildings were declared a Recognized Federal Heritage Building in 1989, in part due to its Art Deco style.

Description: White tower

Location: Port Weller

Directions: From Port Weller, head north on Welland Canals Parkway from Lakeshore Rd to a parking lot at 1.6 km. Continue on foot for 1.6 km along the pier trail. The lighthouse is at the tip

Coordinates: 43°14'41.2"N 79°13'03.2"W

Opened: 1931

Automated: 1969

Deactivated: Active

Lens: Sixth-order dioptric

Height: 95 feet (29 metres)

Focal Height: 40 feet (12.2 metres)

Signal: White flash every 5 seconds

Foghorn Signal: Two blasts a minute

Visitor Access: Closed

Queen's Wharf Lighthouse, Golden Horseshoe Region

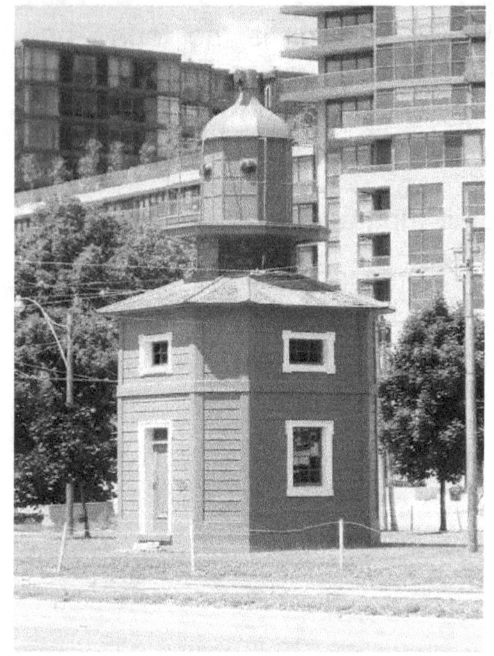

This lighthouse currently sits at a distance from Lake Ontario but this area was once known as the Queen's Wharf, a pier that situated into the Toronto Harbour. This pier was named the Queen's Wharf.

The building was constructed in 1861. After a safer new western channel was opened, it became redundant and was deactivated in 1912.

The structure was moved 30 feet (9 metres) in 1901 in an effort to improve dredging operations at the pier. In 1929 the building was again moved about 1500 feet (450 metres) after being deactivated. This area had been filled in by the railways to provide space for tracks and facilities.

The building was listed in the Toronto Heritage Register on June 20, 1973. In 1988, restoration work was done by the Historical Board of Toronto.

Location: Toronto

Directions: Fleet Street just east of the Princes' Gates at Exhibition Place

Coordinates: 43.635889°N 79.404972°W

Opened: 1861

Automated: 1938

Deactivated: 1912

Height: 36 Metres (11 Feet)

Signal: Red Light (Not active)

Visitor Access: Grounds open, interior closed

Toronto Harbour Lighthouse, Golden Horseshoe Region

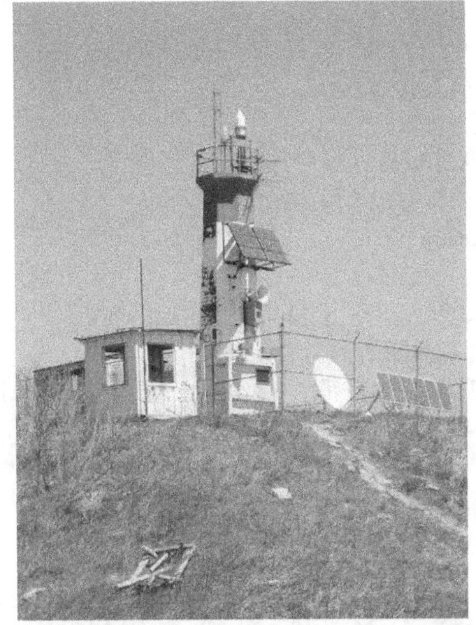

Tommy Thompson Park tip is the site of the Toronto Harbour Light. The area is famous among bird lovers as a productive place to visit during migration. It was artificially created by the Toronto Harbour Commission to serve shipping needs which were thought would be required with the opening of the Saint Lawrence Seaway. When it was clear that it would not be needed for this purpose, there were different proposals, including building a resort with various facilities. The Friends of the Spit group formed to promote a public park left in a natural state and were successful. Tommy Thompson Park was formed in 1985.

The Toronto Harbour Commission established a light on a tower at the tip in 1974. It is powered by a solar panel and orients shipping to the Eastern Channel of Toronto Harbour

The entrance to Tommy Thompson Park (Also known as the Leslie St Spit) is at the intersection of Unwin Ave and Leslie St. The trail can be used by walking or biking and the Light is at the tip. Total round trip is 10 km. in easy conditions

Location: Toronto

Directions: Tommy Thompson Park trail to the tip

Coordinates: 43°36'54.0"N 79°20'36.4"W

Opened: 1974

Automated: 1974

Deactivated: Active

Height: 40 feet (12.2 metres)

Focal Height: 74 feet (22.6 metres)

Signal: Red flash every ten seconds

Visitor Access: The park is open on weekends and some holidays

Other Golden Horseshoe Region Lighthouses

Name: Port Colborne Outer
Description: White square tower, red upper
Directions: Accessible by boat
Automated: 1986
Height: 25 feet (7.7 metres)
Signal: Fixed red
Coordinates: 42°51'45.4"N 79°15'17.6"W
Location: Port Colborne
Opened: 1928
Deactivated: Active
Focal Height: 36 feet (11 metres)
Access: Closed

Name: Port Colborne Inner
Description: White square tower, red upper
Directions: Accessible by boat
Automated: 1986
Height: 43 feet (13.1 metres)
Signal: White flash every 10 seconds
Access: Closed
Coordinates: 42°52'03.3"N 79°15'09.9"W
Location: Port Colborne
Opened: 1903
Deactivated: Active
Focal Height: 50 feet (15.2 metres)
Foghorn Signal: 2.5 sec. blast once minute

Name: Toronto East Entrance Inner
Description: Wooden, pyramidal tower
Directions: 300 Humber Bay Park Rd W
Automated: 1937
Height: 22 feet (6.7 metres)
Access: Closed
Coordinates: 43°36'52.9"N 79°28'59.8"W
Location: Toronto
Opened: 1906
Deactivated: 1973
Foghorn Signal: 7 sec blast every 45 sec
Note: Moved to Mimico Cruising Club

Name: Toronto East Entrance Outer
Description: Wooden, pyramidal tower
Directions: 300 Humber Bay Park Rd W
Automated: 1937
Foghorn Signal: 7 sec blast every 45 sec
Note: Moved to Etobicoke Yacht Club
Coordinates: 43°37'05.2"N 79°28'53.3"W
Location: Toronto
Opened: 1906
Deactivated: 1973
Access: Closed

Battle Island Lighthouse, Northwestern Ontario Region

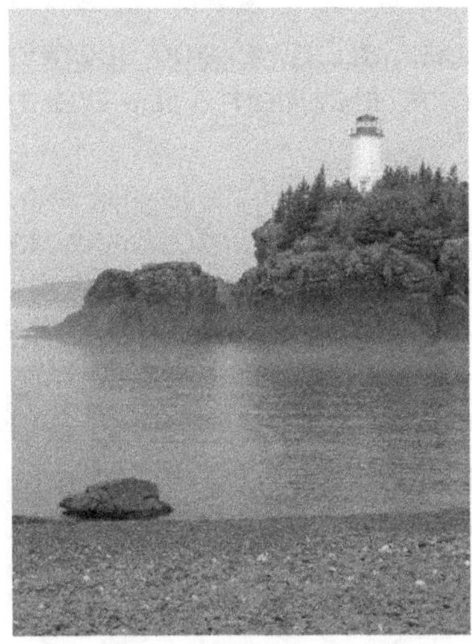

The original light on Battle Island opened in 1877. Its first keeper was Charles McKay who held the post for 36 years. His son, Edward McKay, served for the next 9 years. This period saw the replacement of the original lighthouse.

In 1915 the present lighthouse replaced the original 1877 wooden structure. Additionally, a foghorn was added, with a separate dwelling and a separate keeper.

It was designated as a Federal Heritage Building on June 27, 1991.

Description: White octagonal tower with red top

Location: Battle Island off Rossport, Lake Superior

Directions: Accessible by boat

Coordinates: 48°45'06.4"N 87°33'24.4"W

Opened: 1915

Automated: 1991

Deactivated: Active

Lens: Long-focus reflector

Height: 43 feet (13.1 metres)

Focal Height: 118 feet (36 metres)

Signal: Flash white at 10 second intervals

Foghorn Signal: Blast with 9 second eclipse

Visitor Access: Grounds open, interior closed

Caribou Island Lighthouse, Northwestern Ontario Region

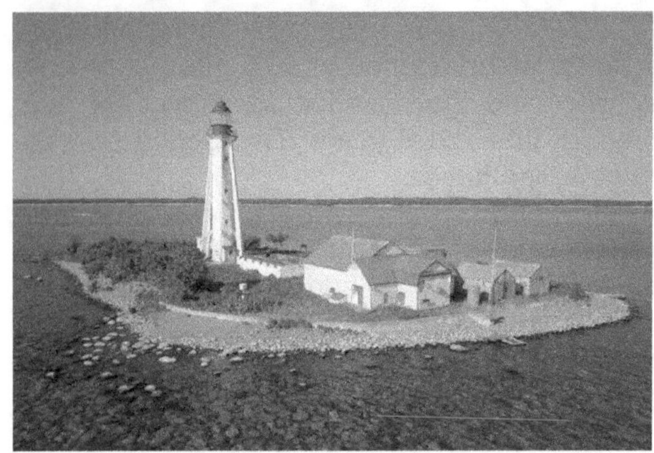

The first lighthouse on Caribou Island opened in in 1886. The station included a fog-alarm building.

Caribou island Lighthouse is the most remote on Lake Superior and has been dangerous for the keepers coming and going from the site. This problem was exacerbated in 1915 when the government stopped delivering and retrieving the keepers, but instead provided a sailboat for their use. Two keepers were lost before the policy was rescinded.

In 1910 the fog alarm was upgraded and in 1911 a new lighthouse was built. It is a beautiful tall white tower with flying buttresses.

Description: White hexagonal tower with red lantern room

Location: Off Caribou Island

Directions: Accessible by boat

Coordinates: 47°20'22.5"N 85°49'33.0"W

Opened: 1912

Automated: 1968

Deactivated: Active

Lens: Second-order Fresnel

Height: 99 feet (30 metres)

Focal Height: 104 feet (31.6 metres)

Signal: White flash every 10 seconds

Foghorn Signal: 5 seconds blast every 30 seconds

Visitor Access: Grounds open, interior closed

Gros Cap Reefs Light, Northwestern Ontario Region

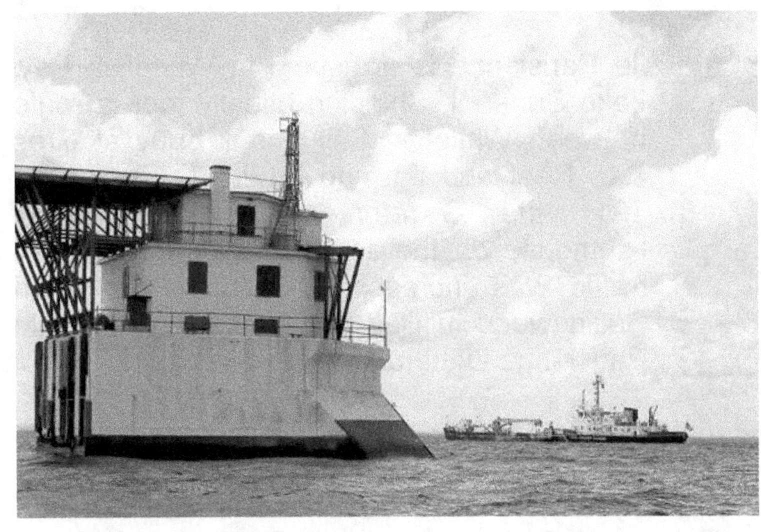

The Gros Cap Reefs are located near the U.S-Canada border and both countries have recognized the danger these reefs have to shipping.

A World War One trawler called the St. Julien was decommissioned and repurposed as Gros Cap Reefs Light-vessel No. 22 in 1923. It served this task for 29 years, being retired in 1952.

The Gros Cap Reef Lighthouse was built onto a crib, towed into place and the crib filled with rocks. It began operations in 1953

Description: White tower

Location: Sault Ste. Marie

Directions: Accessible by boat

Coordinates: 46°30'43.7"N 84°36'54.9"W

Opened: 1953

Automated: 1980

Deactivated: Active

Height: 60 feet (18.3 metres)

Focal Height: 59 feet (18.1 metres)

Signal: White flash every 10 seconds

Foghorn signal; Blast every 10 seconds

Visitor Access: Closed

Ile Parisienne Light, Northwestern Ontario Region

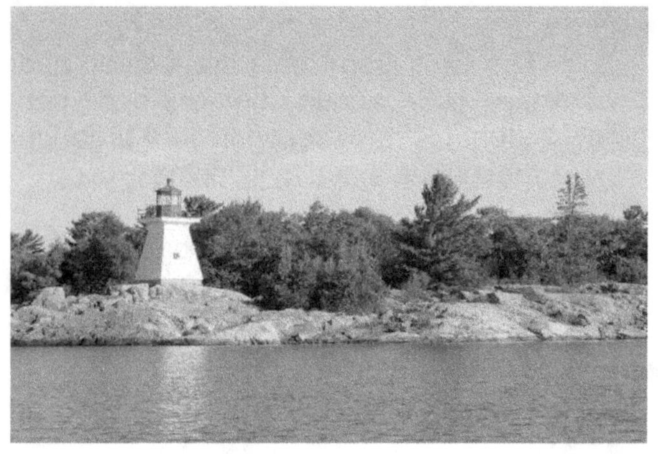

Ile Parisienne is an island in Whitefish Bay, Lake Superior. Shipping usually took a route between Whitefish Bay and a buoy at Gros Cap Reef and passing by Ile Parisienne. In 1911 the Government tendered for a lighthouse on the south tip of the island as traffic was increasing. William Fryer from Collingwood fulfilled this contract and the Ile Parisienne Lighthouse opened in 1912.

In April 1922 a major disaster occurred to Lake Superior lighthouse keepers. The steamship Lambton made her first trip of the year into Lake Superior with 22 crew, 3 lighthouse keepers and two assistants who served Parisienne Island; Caribou Island and Michipicoten Island. She was caught in a storm and was lost with all aboard 75 miles north of Sault Ste Marie. John Douglas, the first Keeper at Ile Parisienne Lighthouse was one of the ill-fated men. No bodies were ever recovered from the cold depths of Lake Superior. In 1991 Ile Parisienne Lighthouse was declared a Recognized Federal Heritage Building.

Description: Hexagonal gray tower with buttresses

Location: Ile Parisienne

Directions: Accessible by boat

Coordinates: 46.645278°N 84.724°W

Opened: 1911

Deactivated: Active

Height: 54 feet (16.6 metres)

Focal Height: 53 feet (16.1 metres)

Signal: White light, four seconds lit and two seconds eclipse

Foghorn Signal: 1 second blast, 9 seconds eclipse

Visitor Access: No access

Janet Head Lighthouse, Northwestern Ontario Region

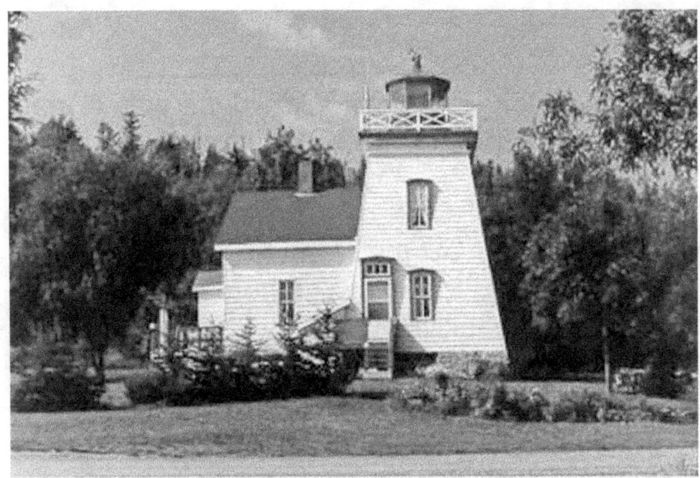

In 1879, the Janet Head Lighthouse opened. A keeper's dwelling is attached to the tower.

In 1988, a fog horn was added to the station.

The station is still active with a light which operates the full day.

It is also known as the Gore Bay Lighthouse.

Description: White square tower with red upper portion

Location: Manitoulin Island

Directions: From Gore Bay, head northeast on Lighthouse Rd/Water St for 3.2 km where you will find the lighthouse

Coordinates: 45°56'45.0"N 82°28'48.6"W

Opened: 1879

Automated: 1955

Deactivated: Active

Lens: Seventh-order dioptric

Height: 35 feet (10.6 metres)

Focal Height: 49 feet (15 metres)

Signal: 3 second white flash followed by 2 second eclipse

Visitor Access: Grounds open, interior open during July and August

Kagawong Lighthouse, Northwestern Ontario Region

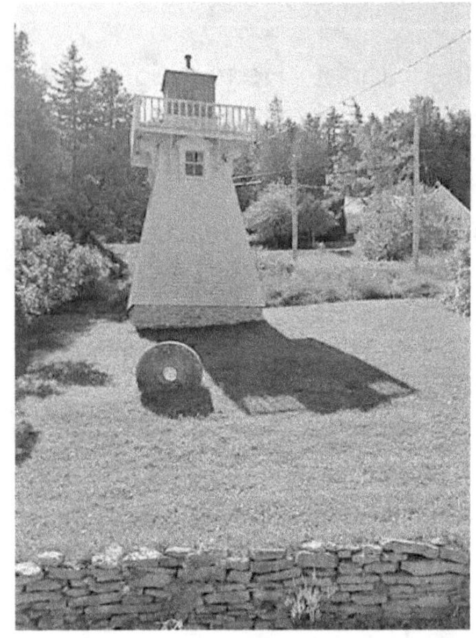

The first light at Kagawong on Manitoulin Island was a mast which opened in 1888. However it was destroyed in a fire in 1892.

In 1894 the Department of the Marine supervised the construction of a square tapered lighthouse tower. This lighthouse continues to be active

Description: White square tapered wooden tower

Location: Kagawong

Directions: From Younge St/ON-540 E in Kagawong, head northwest on Main St for 0.9 km where you will find the lighthouse

Coordinates: 45°54'35.6"N 82°15'37.4"W

Opened: 1894

Automated: 1960

Deactivated: Active

Lens: Catoptric

Height: 31 feet (9.4 metres)

Focal Height: 44 feet (13.4 metres)

Signal: Fixed red

Visitor Access: Grounds open, interior closed

Manitowaning Lighthouse, Northwestern Ontario Region

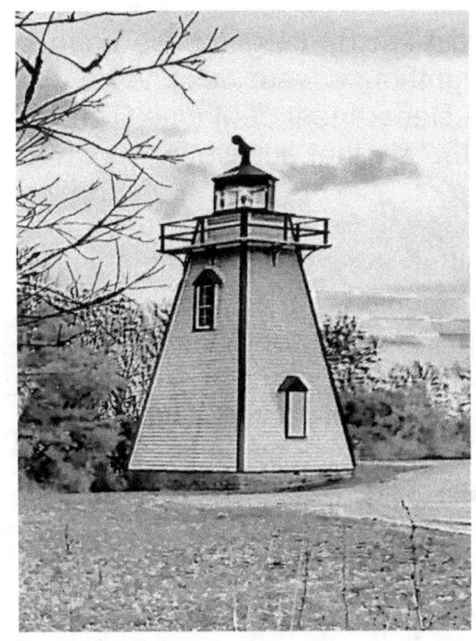

In 1884, J. Waddell of Kingston won a contract to build five lighthouse by the Department of Marine, including the Manitowaning Lighthouse. When he failed to complete it, the Department of Marine stood in to finish it and it opened in 1885.

The tower was repaired by the Coast Guard in 1995. This included replacing beams and shingling.

Description: Square tapered wooden tower

Location: Manitowaning, Manitoulin Island

Directions: 198 Arthur St, Manitowaning

Coordinates: 45°44'41.4"N 81°48'18.5"W

Opened: 1885

Automated: 1964

Deactivated: Active

Height: 34 feet (10.4 metres)

Focal Height: 80 feet (24.4 metres)

Signal: Fixed green

Visitor Access: Grounds open, interior closed

Michipicoten Island East End Lighthouse, Northwestern Ontario Region

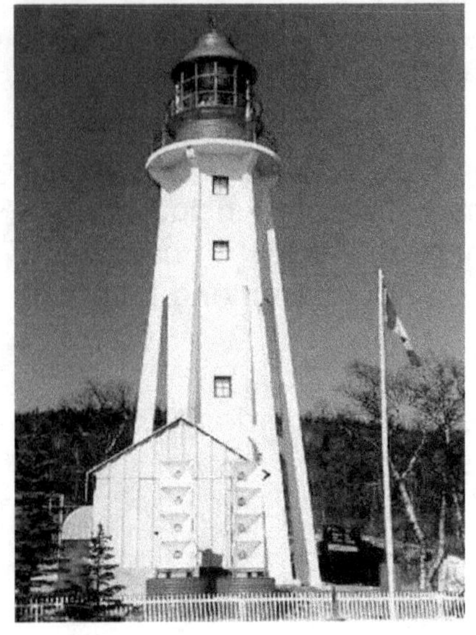

In 1912 the Michipicoten Island East End Lighthouse opened operations. It and eight other lighthouse were designed by W. Anderson, an engineer with the Department of Marine. They all featured flying buttresses and the six that survive are both tall and beautiful.

In 1915, Keepers were told that they would no longer be transported to and from their stations, but were issued a sailboat to make the journey. In 1916 Keeper William Sherlock and his son James barely survived a journey of eighty days to reach the mainland. In 1916, they set out and were never seen again. Other keepers lost their lives as well and the government wisely reversed their policy.

A diaphone fog alarm was added in 1953 which gave a two second blast every thirty seconds.

Description: White concrete tower with buttresses

Location: Wawa

Directions: Best seen by boat

Coordinates: 47°45'13.3"N 85°35'48.5"W

Opened: 1912

Automated: 1988

Deactivated: Active

Lens: Third-order Fresnel

Height: 83 feet (25.3 metres)

Focal Height: 84 feet (25.6 metres)

Signal: White flash every 10 seconds

Foghorn Signal: Two-second blast every thirty seconds

Visitor Access: Grounds open, interior closed

Mississagi Strait Lighthouse, Northwestern Ontario Region

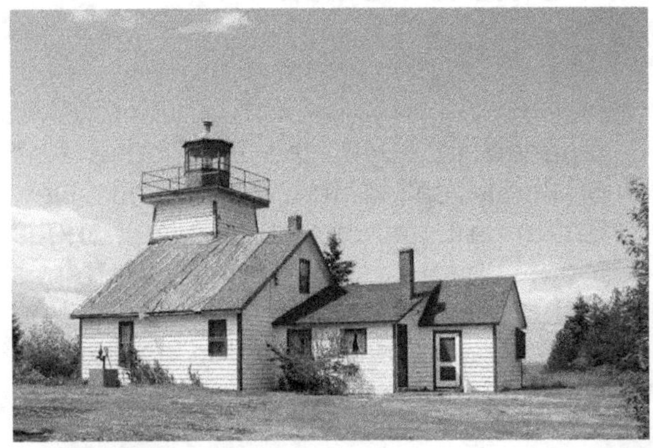

The initial 1855 contract for the Imperial Towers include a lighthouse to be built at Mississagi Strait. However, cost overruns eliminated it. The station was finally built in 1873 with John Miller as the first keeper. In 1881, a foghorn was added. It was gradually upgraded and in 1906 a state of the art foghorn was in use. In 1908, repairs and improvements were completed. This included replacing the reflector system with a fourth-order Fresnel lens.

The station is currently a museum operated by the Manitoulin Tourism Association. The building and lighthouse were recognized as a Federal Heritage Building on March 31st, 1994.

Description: Square tower attached to the Keeper's dwelling

Location: Manitoulin Island

Directions: In the west part of Manitoulin Island, take Mississagi Lighthouse Rd off Hyway 540 for 6.6 km and turn left to stay on Mississagi Lighthouse Rd. Continue for 6.5 km and turn right where you will find the lighthouse.

Coordinates: 45°53'29.5"N 83°13'32.5"W

Opened: 1873

Automated: 1970

Deactivated: Active

Lens: Fourth-order Fresnel

Height: 28 feet (8.5 metres)

Focal Height: 46 feet (14 metres)

Signal: White flash for 2 seconds followed by 2 second eclipse

Foghorn Signal: Three-second blasts every forty-five seconds

Visitor Access: Ground open, lighthouse open seasonly.

Thunder Bay Main Lighthouse, Northwestern Ontario Region

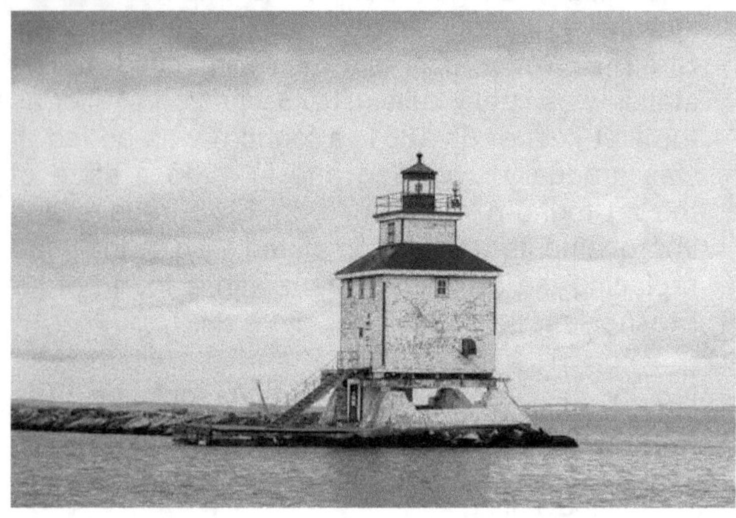

Opened in 1940, the lighthouse was originally called the Port Arthur New Entrance Lighthouse but was changed to Thunder Bay Central Entrance Lighthouse when Port Arthur and Fort William were amalgamated as the city of Thunder Bay in 1970.

The station was out of commission for several months after a Lake Freighter ran into the breakwater in 1971.

Description: White square tower

Location: Thunder Bay

Directions: On detached breakwater off downtown Thunder Bay

Coordinates: 48°25'57.3"N 89°11'45.8"W

Opened: 1940

Automated: 1979

Deactivated: Active

Lens: Catoptric

Height: 31 feet (9.4 metres)

Focal Height: 49 feet (14.9 metres)

Signal: Red flash every 5 seconds

Foghorn Signal: 3 blasts per minute

Visitor Access: Grounds open, interior closed

Name: Angus Island
Coordinates: 48°14'07.7"N 89°00'26.2"W
Description: Skeleton tower
Location: Angus Island
Directions: Accessible by boat
Opened: 1927
Automated: 1988
Deactivated: Active
Height: 52 feet (15.9 metres)
Focal Height: 81 feet (24.7 metres)
Signal: White flash every 10 seconds
Foghorn Signal: Blast 2.5 sec twice a minute
Access: Grounds open, interior closed

Name: Coppermine Point
Coordinates: 47°00'42.1"N 84°46'29.7"W
Description: Cylindrical mast
Location: Coppermine Point
Directions: From Pancake Bay P.P. go north on Trans Canada Highway for 11 km where you find the lighthouse
Opened: 1908
Automated: 1923
Deactivated: 1960s
Height: 18 feet (5.5 metres)
Focal Height: 47 feet (14.4 metres)
Signal: White flash every 4 seconds
Access: Grounds open, interior closed

Name: Corbeil Point
Coordinates: 46°53'20.8"N 84°36'56.4"W
Description: Square, two-storey dwelling
Location: Corbeil Point
Directions: From the Trans-Canada Highway north of Sault Sainte Marie, turn left on and in ON-563 7.7 km you will find the lighthouse
Opened: 1932
Automated: 1955
Deactivated: 1962
Focal Height: 43 feet (13.1 metres)
Signal: Fixed green
Access: Closed
Note: Currently a private residence

Name: Davieaux Island
Coordinates: 47°41'41.2"N 85°48'41.6"W
Description: White concrete octagonal tower
Location: Davieaux Island
Directions: Accessible by boat
Opened: 1918
Automated: 1968
Deactivated: Active
Lens: Catoptric
Height: 44 feet (13.4 metres)
Focal Height: 92 feet (28 metres)
Signal: White flash every twenty seconds
Foghorn Signal: Blast every eight seconds
Access: Grounds open, interior closed

Name: Great Duck Island
Coordinates: 45°38'33.2"N 82°57'45.4"W
Description: White octagonal tower
Location: South Baymouth
Directions: Accessible by boat
Opened: 1877
Automated: 1987
Deactivated: Active
Lens: Reflectors
Height: 85 feet (25.9 metres)
Focal Height: 108 feet (32.9 metres)
Signal: White flash every 10 seconds
Foghorn Signal: 2.5 sec Blast, 30 sec eclipse
Access: Closed

Name: Lamb Island
Coordinates: 48°36'12.2"N 88°08'34.4"W
Description: Square, skeletal tower
Location: Lamb Island
Directions: Accessible by boat
Opened: 1961
Automated: 1989
Deactivated: Active
Lens: Fourth-order Fresnel
Height: 44 feet (13.6 metres)
Focal Height: 99 feet (30.2 metres)
Signal: White flash every 5 seconds
Access: Grounds open, interior closed

Name: Little Current
Coordinates: 45°58'49.9"N 81°55'20.1"W
Description: Square wooden tower
Location: Little Current
Directions: 39 Water St E, Little Current
Opened: 2012 (Replica)
Lens: Catoptric
Height: 22 feet (6.7 metres)
Signal: Fixed white
Access: Grounds open, tower closed

Name: Lonely Island
Coordinates: 45°34'25.3"N 81°28'05.2"W
Description: White octagonal tower
Location: Lonely Island
Directions: Accessible by boat
Opened: 1907
Automated: 1987
Deactivated: Active
Lens: Third-order Fresnel
Height: 46 feet (13.9 metres)
Focal Height: 195 feet (59.4 metres)
Signal: White flash every 10 seconds
Access: Closed

Name: McKay Island
Coordinates: 46°16'56.0"N 83°46'51.4"W
Description: Skeleton tower
Location: McKay Island
Directions: From Trans-Canada Hwy at Bruce Mines, go south on Bruce Bay Rd for 1.8 km. Continue onto French Island Rd where the lighthouse is 1.1 km
Opened: 1907
Automated: 1955
Deactivated: Active
Lens: Dioptric
Height: 32 feet (9.8 metres)
Focal Height: 42 feet (12.7 metres)
Signal: White flash every 4 seconds
Access: Grounds open, tower open to guests

Name: Michael's Bay
Coordinates: 45°34'35.4"N 82°07'40.0"W
Description: White octagonal tapered tower
Location: South Baymouth
Directions: Best seen by boat
Opened: 1870
Deactivated: 1907
Lens: Catoptric
Height: 22 feet (6.7 metres)
Access: Grounds open, interior closed
Note: Collapsed in 1947, rebuilt by volunteers in 2005

Name: Michipicoten Harbour
Coordinates: 47°56'32.9"N 84°54'26.7"W
Description: Skeletal tower
Location: Wawa
Directions: Best seen by boat
Opened: 1967
Automated: 1983
Deactivated: Active
Lens: Dioptric of the seventh order
Height: 42 feet (12.7 metres)
Focal Height: 88 feet (26.8 metres)
Signal: White flash every 10 seconds
Access: Grounds open, interior closed

Name: Otter Island
Coordinates: 48°06'42.2"N 86°04'00.3"W
Description: White hexagonal tower
Location: Otter Island
Directions: Accessible by boat
Opened: 1903
Automated: 1987
Deactivated: Active
Lens: Reflector
Height: 21 feet (6.3 metres)
Focal Height: 97 feet (29.6 metres)
Signal: White flash every 10 seconds
Foghorn Signal: 2 second blast each minute
Access: Grounds open, interior closed

Name: Pie Island
Coordinates: 48°13'40.9"N 89°10'28.5"W
Description: Skeleton tower
Location: Pie Island
Directions: Best seen by boat
Opened: 1953
Automated: 1953
Deactivated: Active
Lens: Dioptric of the seventh order
Height: 20 feet (6.1 metres)
Focal Height: 27 feet (8.3 metres)
Signal: White flash every 4 seconds
Access: Grounds open, interior closed

Name: Providence Bay
Coordinates: 45°39'05.0"N 82°16'32.0"W
Description: Skeleton tower
Location: Manitoulin Island
Directions: From Providence Bay, head south on ON-551 S and turn left at the 3rd cross street onto Mira St/ON-551 S. Continue 2.7 km where you find the lighthouse
Opened: 1973
Automated: 1973
Height: 42 feet (12.8 metres)
Focal Height: 43 feet (13.1 metres)
Access: Grounds open, interior closed

Name: Pointe aux Pins Range Front
Coordinates: 46°28'03.9"N 84°28'20.7"W
Description: Square tower, red daymark
Location: Sault Ste. Marie
Directions: Best viewed by boat
Opened: 1903
Automated: 1966
Height: 34 feet (10.5 metres)
Deactivated: Active
Lens: Fourth-order Fresnel
Focal Height: 40 feet (12.3 metres)
Signal: Fixed red
Access: Closed

Name: Pointe aux Pins Range Rear
Description: Square tower, red daymark
Directions: Best viewed by boat
Automated: 1983
Height: 55 feet (16.8 metres)
Signal: Fixed red
Coordinates: 46°27'55.7"N 84°28'26.7"W
Location: Sault Ste. Marie
Opened: 1983
Deactivated: Active
Focal Height: 63 feet (19.1 metres)
Access: Closed

Name: Porphyry Point
Description: Square, pyramidal
Directions: Accessible by boat
Automated: 1979
Lens: Fourth-order Fresnel
Focal Height: 82 feet (25 metres)
Access: Closed
Coordinates: 48°20'20.9"N 88°38'55.3"W
Location: Porphyry Island
Opened: 1960
Deactivated: Active
Height: 60 feet (18.3 metres)
Signal: Flashing white

Name: Shaganash Island
Description: White tower with red top
Directions: Accessible by boat
Automated: 1954
Lens: Fifth-order Fresnel
Signal: White flash every 4 seconds
Coordinates: 48°26'09.3"N 88°28'50.9"W
Location: Shaganash island No. 10
Opened: 1923
Deactivated: Active
Focal Height: 36 feet (11 meters)
Access: Grounds open, interior close

Name: Shoal Island
Coordinates: 46°18'48.1"N 84°04'32.3"W
Description: White square tower
Location: Shoal Island
Directions: From Richard's Landing, had west on Russell St/ON-548 for 1.8 km and turn right onto B Line Rd to the end. The lighthouse is just offshore
Opened: 1909
Deactivated: Active
Height: 31 feet (9.5 metres)
Signal: White flash every 4 seconds
Automated: 1954
Lens: Seventh-order Fresnel
Focal Height: 37 feet (11 metres)
Access: Closed

Name: Slate islands
Description: White octagonal tower
Directions: Accessible by boat
Automated: 1989
Height: 34 feet (10.5 metres)
Signal: 2 white flashes every fifteen seconds
Access: Grounds open, interior closed
Coordinates: 48°37'19.3"N 86°59'43.0"W
Location: Slate Islands
Opened: 1903
Deactivated: Active
Focal Height: 224 feet (68.3 metres)
Foghorn Signal: 3.5 second blast per minute

Name: South Baymouth Range Front
Coordinates: 45°33'27.7"N 82°00'47.9"W
Description: White square structure
Location: South Baymouth
Directions: Across from ferry terminal
Opened: 1898
Automated: 1958
Deactivated: Active
Lens: Dioptric of the seventh order
Height: 26 feet (8 metres)
Focal Height: 28 feet (8.5 metres)
Signal: Fixed Green
Foghorn Signal: 2.5 blast twice minute
Access: Grounds open, interior closed

Name: South Baymouth Range Rear
Coordinates: 45°33'33.1"N 82° 0'44.6"W
Description: White square structure
Location: South Baymouth
Directions: 56 Water St., South Baymouth
Opened: 1898
Automated: 1958
Deactivated: Active
Lens: Catoptric
Height: 36 feet (10.9 metres)
Focal Height: 46 feet (14 metres)
Signal: Fixed Green
Foghorn Signal: 2.5 blast twice minute
Access: Closed

Name: Strawberry Island
Coordinates: 45°58'24.6"N 81°51'15.1"W
Description: White tower
Location: Strawberry Island
Directions: Best seen by boat
Opened: 1881
Automated: 1966
Deactivated: Active
Lens: Fourth-order Fresnel
Height: 40 feet (12.3 metres)
Focal Height: 58 feet (14.6 metres)
Signal: White flash every 4 seconds
Access: Closed

Name: Tomahawk Island
Coordinates: 49°01'35.1"N 94°23'53.0"W
Description: Cylindrical mast
Location: Lake of the Woods
Location: Lake of the Woods
Directions: North on Lighthouse Rd from Hwy 621 for 3.2 km
Opened: 1962
Automated: 1962
Deactivated: Active
Height: 21 feet (6.4 metres)
Focal Height: 32 feet (9.8 metres)
Signal: Green flash every 4 seconds
Access: Grounds open, interior closed

Name: Trowbridge Island
Coordinates: 48°17'32.3"N 88°52'30.3"W
Description: White octagonal tower
Location: Trowbridge Island
Directions: Accessible by boat
Opened: 1924
Automated: 1988
Deactivated: Active
Lens: Third-order Fresnel
Height: 38 feet (11.5 metres)
Focal Height: 114 feet (34.7 metres)
Signal: White flash every 5 seconds
Foghorn Signal: 3.25 sec blast every minute
Access: Grounds open, interior closed

Name: Welcome Island

Coordinates: 48°22'09.4"N 89°07'10.8"W
Description: Skeleton tower
Location: Welcome Island
Directions: Accessible by boat
Opened: 1959
Automated: 1985
Deactivated: Active
Lens: Fourth-order Fresnel
Focal Height: 138 feet (42 metres)
Signal: White flash every 10 seconds
Foghorn Signal: Two blasts each 70 seconds
Access: Closed

Name: West Sister Rock

Coordinates: 46°18'13.6"N 83°54'56.6"W
Description: White, hexagonal tower
Location: Thunder Bay
Directions: Accessible by boat
Opened: 1885
Automated: 1951
Deactivated: Active
Height: 32 feet (9.7 metres)
Focal Height: 38 feet (11.7 metres)
Signal: White flash every 4 seconds
Access: Closed

Big Tub Lighthouse (Tobermory), Eastern Ontario Region

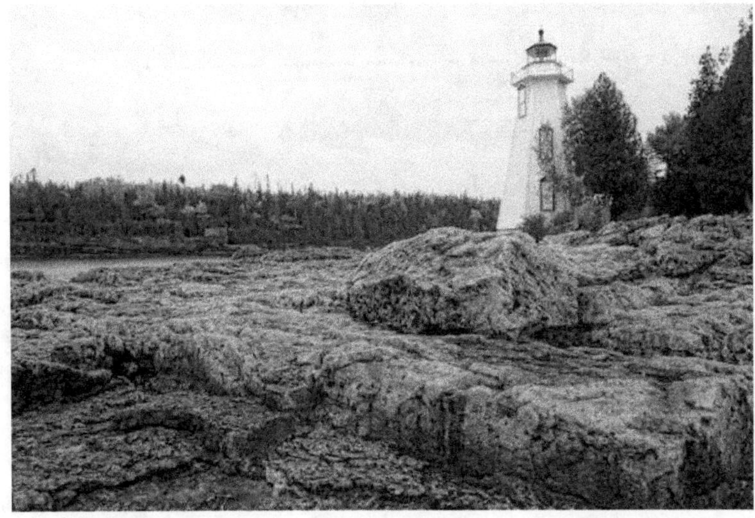

Tobermory Harbour was often used as a sanctuary by ships in bad weather but it was difficult to find and navigate the entrance. In early years a man was paid to hang a lantern on a tree branch. While this was no doubt occasionally useful, it it did not provide the needed level of safety. A recommendation was made by the Commissioners of Public Works in 1857 for a Lighthouse at Tobermory but it was over 25 years before it was acted on. John George and David Currie were hired to raise this building for the sum of $675.

Abraham Davis was made the first permanent Keeper in 1885. In 1895 he disappeared and was presumed drowned after taking a small boat to visit the site of a wrecked vessel. Many people expressed support for his widow, Flora Davis, to continue his job as she was familiar with the work, and had apparently been engaged in it when her husband still lived. However the officials in charge refused to appoint a woman to the post, but instead appointed her son, Henry Davis. In 1898 complaints were made that Henry Davis had farmed the job out to Henry Martin while retaining a quarter of the pay. Keeper Davis protested but resigned shortly thereafter.

A foghorn was added to station equipment in 1910.The light was electrified and and automated in 1952. In 1929 a fourth-order lens upgraded the lighting equipment . It continues to shine each night.

Big Tub Lighthouse became a Recognized Federal Heritage Building on April 30, 1992.

Description: White hexagonal tower

Location: Tobermory

Directions: From Highway 6 in Tobermory, go west on Big Tub Rd which loops back to the east where you find the lighthouse in 2.2 km.

Coordinates: 45°15′27″N 81°40′22″W

Opened: 1885

Automated: 1952

Deactivated: Still active

Lens: Fourth-order Fresnel

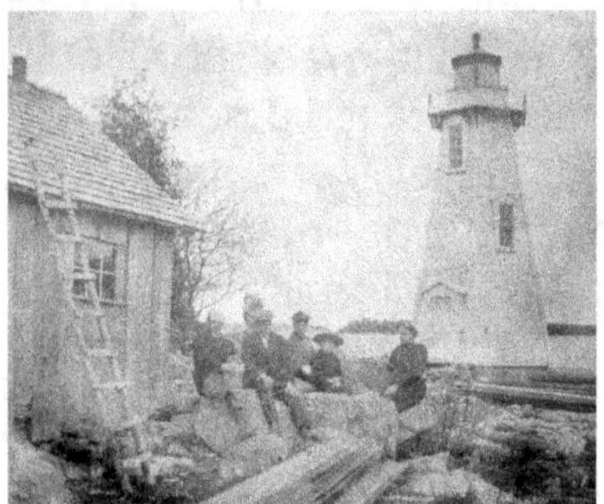
Courtesy Library and Archives Canada

Height: 41 feet (12.5 metres)

Focal Height: 43 feet (13 metres)

Signal: Fixed red

Visitor Access: Grounds open, interior closed

Bois Blanc Island Lighthouse, Southwestern Ontario Region

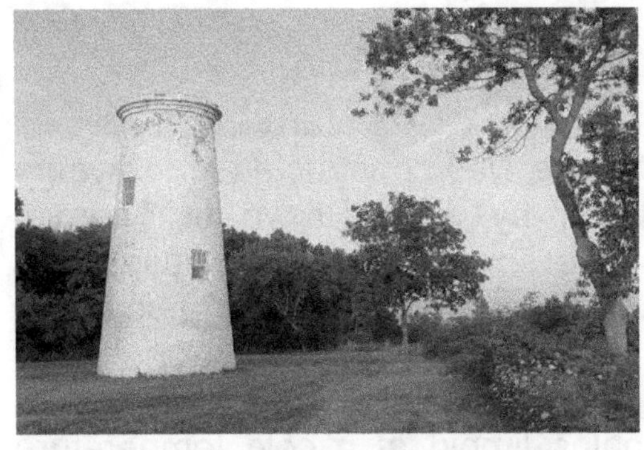

In 1835 commissioners were appointed to advice as to where to locate a a lighthouse at the Lake Erie entrance to the Detroit River. They recommended its placement on Bois Blanc Island at the south end. John Cook was the winning bidder for the contract tendered by the Parliament of Upper Canada. He successfully fulfilled the contact and the Bois Blanc Island Lighthouse opened in 1836. It is the third lighthouse to be built on Lake Erie. From the 1836 opening until the automation in 1924, the lighthouse keepers were various members of the Hackett family. James Hackett was the initial keeper, serving until 1870, when his son, Andrew Hackett assumed the duties. After Andrew's death in 1901, his widow Agnes Hackett carried on until 1910. Charles Hackett, her son, became the final keeper, serving until 1924.

In 1838, members of the Upper Canada Rebellion raided the island, but they were quickly forced out and captured. Defensive blockhouses were constructed in 1939.

Parks Canada performed restoration work to the tower Ca. 1970. The lighthouse and blockhouses were given an Historic Designation on May 10, 1955.

Description: White tapered cylindrical tower

Location: Amherstburg

Directions: From Amherstburg, you can take a ferry to Bois Blance Island, and the walk to the lighthouse is 1.4 km.

Coordinates: 42°05'13.1"N 83°07'10.1"W

Opened: 1836

Automated: 1924

Deactivated: 1959

Lens: Fourth-order Fresnel

Height: 39 feet (12 metres)

Signal: Fixed white

Visitor Access: Grounds open, interior closed

Chantry Island Lighthouse, Southwestern Ontario Region

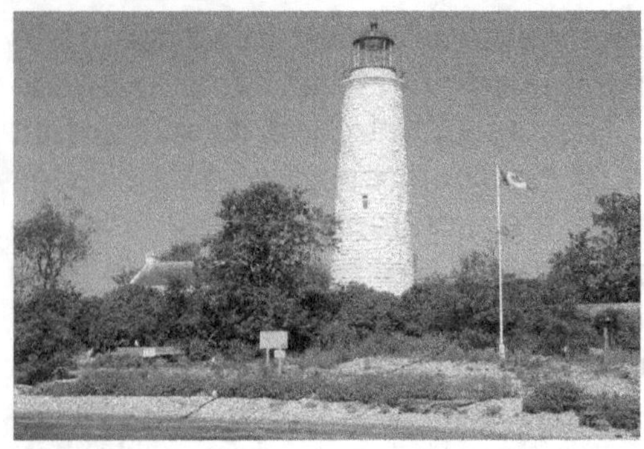

Chantry Island Lighthouse was constructed in the years 1855 through to 1859, by John Brown of Thorold, Ontario. It is one of the six Imperial Lighthouses. For more information on them, see the article on page 9.

Whale oil was burned in the tower's lamps initially but colza oil, which remains limpid at a cold temperature and was less apt to clog the lamps, was introduced in 1860.

Chantry Island Lighthouse was automated in 1954 and has been active since. The island was declared a Federal Migratory Bird Sanctuary in 1957.

The Marine Heritage Society raised over $600,00 in donations to pay for badly needed restoration at the station, particularly the Keeper's dwelling. In 2001, a ceremony was held on completion of the restoration. Much of this work was completed by a large number of volunteers.

The Lighthouse is listed on the National Historic Sites of Canada as of 14 November 1991. The lightkeeper's cottage has a historic designation as well.

Description: White cylindrical tower with red top.

Location: Southampton

Directions: Offshore from Southampton. Although visible from Southampton beach, a boat trip is needed for a close view.

Coordinates: 44.48938°N 81.40194°W

Opened: 1859

Automated: 1954

Deactivated: Active

Lens: Second-order Fresnel

Height: 92 feet (28 metres)

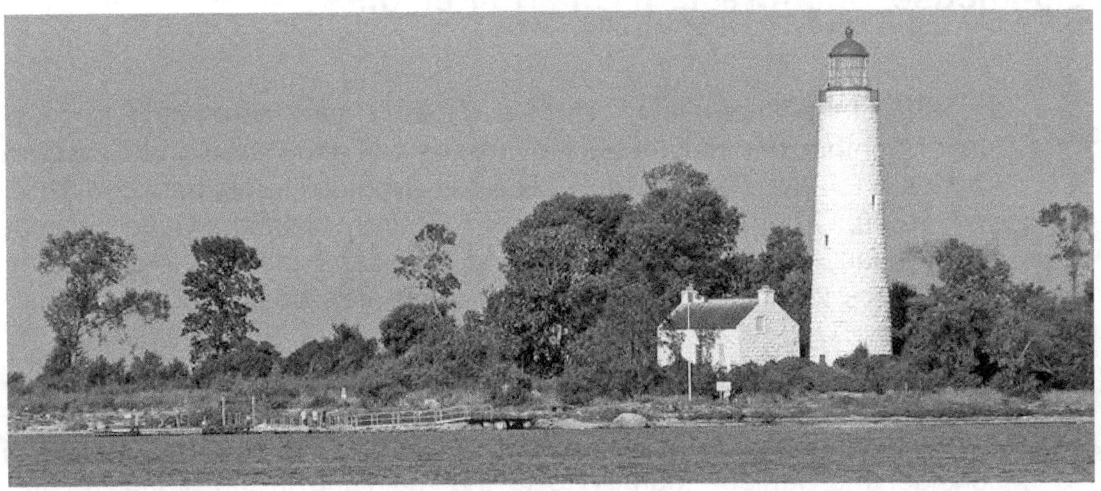

Focal Height: 97 feet (29.5 metres)

Signal: White flash every 4 seconds

Visitor Access: Chantry Island Tours in Southampton offer tours from June to September, including a visit inside the top of the Lighthouse. (Only 107 steps)

Cove Island Lighthouse, Southwestern Ontario Region

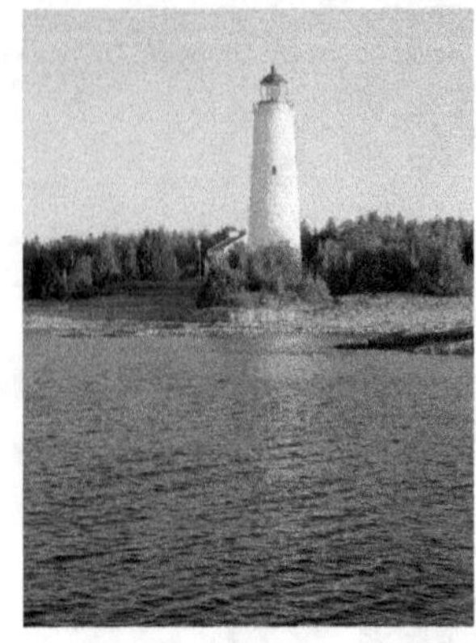

In 1855, John Brown from Thorold, Ontario, was contracted to build eleven lighthouses and keepers' dwellings on Lake Huron and Georgian Bay. Due to cost overruns only six were eventually built between 1855 and 1859. They are Point Clark, Chantry Island, Cove Island, Nottawasaga Island, Griffith Island and Christian Island. As a group they are referred to as the Imperial Towers. See article on page 9.

The Island's keepers have had their share of misadventures. In 1860 Keeper David McBeath and family were waiting for provisions. By early December they were still waiting and were desperate enough to consider the perilous journey to to the mainland in the station's skiff. Captain James Dick of the steamer Rescue arrived in Collinwood harbour on his last voyage of the season. He agreed to deliver the provisions and did so in a bad storm. In later years, Hugh Rumley, Flowerpot Island Lighthouse keeper noticed that the Cove Island light had been absent one night. He quickly went to station where Iris, the Keeper's wife related that her husband had go out to test their new boat and not returned. He was eventually rescued on a small island he had reached after his boat had broken down

A foghorn was added in 1885, powered by steam. The lighthouse can be seen from the ferry from Tobermory to South Baymouth

Location: Cove Island

Directions: Accessible by boat

Coordinates: 45.327080°N 81.735411°W

Opened: 1858

Automated: 1991

Deactivated: Active

Lens: Second-order Fresnel

Height: 80 feet (24 metres)

Focal Height: 103 feet (31.4 metres)

Signal: White flash every 10 seconds

Visitor Access: No access

Goderich Lighthouse, Southwestern Ontario Region

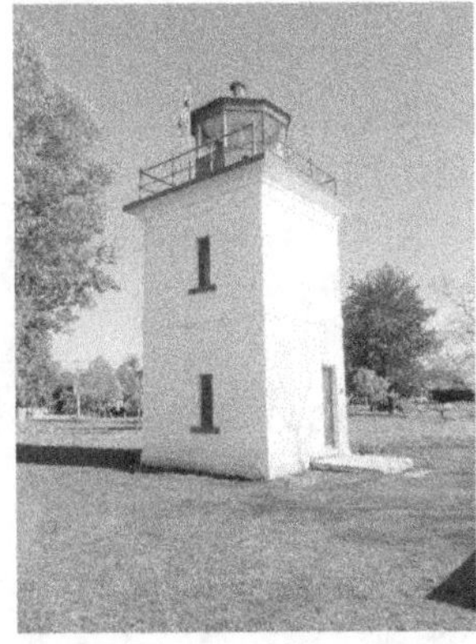

The Lighthouse in Goderich opened in 1847, which makes the structure the oldest lighthouse on Lake Huron. It is also the only Lake Huron lighthouse which is still active. In 1873 a contractor completed a project to provide erosion protection to the bank below the building. Several upgrades have been made to the lighting system with the last being installation of a fourth-order Fresnel lens in 1908.

"The Great Storm of 1913" was the deadliest storm ever recorded on the Great Lakes. Lake Huron was the worst hit with 8 Lake freighters and more than 200 crew lost. At Goderich, the Wexford, fully loaded, went down. An inquiry suggested that the foghorn should have been operated sooner and standardized procedures were needed.

In 1914, the tower was increased by 5 feet and a new lantern was installed. Sometime in the next decade, the kerosene lamp was replaced by an electric light, thus eliminating the need for a full-time light keeper. In 2009, volunteers restored the tower exterior, painting it and replacing doors and windows.

Description: White square tower, red upper portion

Location: Goderich

Directions: 1 Harbour Ln, Goderich

Coordinates: 43.742179°N 81.724564°W

Opened: 1847

Automated: 1993

Deactivated: Active

Lens: Fourth-order Fresnel

Height: 20 feet (6 metres)

Focal Height: 150 feet (46 metres)

Signal: Two white flashes every 25 seconds

Visitor Access: Grounds open, interior closed

Grand Bend Lighthouse, Southwestern Ontario Region

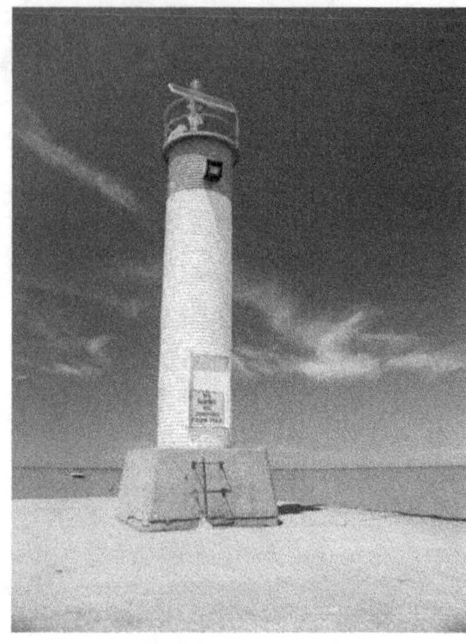

he Grand Bend Lighthouse is located at the mouth of the Ausable River in Grand Bend. The lighthouse opened in 1907 and has had multiple repairs through the years. It is maintained by the Village of Grand Bend.

There is otherwise not a lot of information available about this station.

Description: White cylindrical tower, green upper portion

Location: Grand Bend

Directions: In Grand Bend, head northwest on Main St W from Highway 21, for 0.5 km and turn left on Government Rd. The lighthouse is at the tip of the pier.

Coordinates: 43.313820°N 81.768029°W

Opened: 1907

Automated: Not known

Deactivated: Active (maintained by the municipality of Lambton Shores)

Lens: Not known

Height: 25 feet (7.6 metres)

Focal Height: 19 feet (5.8 metres)

Signal: Green flash every 4 seconds

Foghorn: Blast 3 seconds, silent 27 seconds

Visitor Access: Site open, interior closed

Kincardine Lighthouse, Southwestern Ontario Region

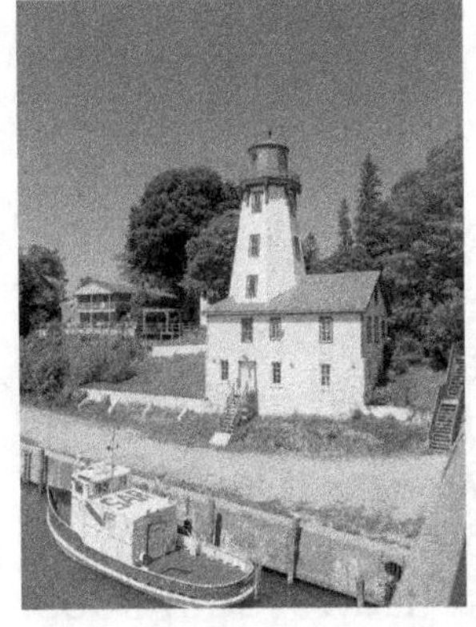

As the Kincardine area began to grow with good farming land as well as developing businesses, it became clear that shipping would be growing as well. The safety of ships would also be important. The harbour was improved through dredging and building of piers. In 1874 the government contracted for a small lighthouse to be built at the tip of the pier. A seven foot high lighthouse was opened the same year.

As expected, shipping grew with a fishing fleet as well as shipping for two salt producing companies. In 1875 an inspection of the lighthouse revealed that both it and the pier were in very poor condition. It was recommended that a new lighthouse replace it.The government approved the new lighthouse which opened in 1881. In 1903 a steam foghorn was added and in 1910, the lighting was upgraded with a fourth-order Fresnel lens. The lighthouse was designated a Heritage Building in 2008.

Description: White octagonal tower, orange rectangular daymark

Location: Kincardine

Directions: In the Town of Kincardine, head northwest on Durham St from Highway 21 for 1.7 km and turn left onto Huron Terrace. In 0.3 km turn right at the 2nd cross street onto Harbour St where you will find the lighthouse

Coordinates: 44.17708°N 81.63809°W

Opened: 1881

Automated: 1977

Deactivated: Active

Lens: Fourth-order Fresnel

Height: 63 feet (19.2 metres)

Focal Height: 80 feet (24.4 metres)

Signal: Red flash every 5 seconds

Foghorn Signal: A two and a half second blast every forty-five seconds

Visitor Access: Open from July 1st through Labour Day

Lion's Head Harbour Lighthouse, Southwestern Ontario Region

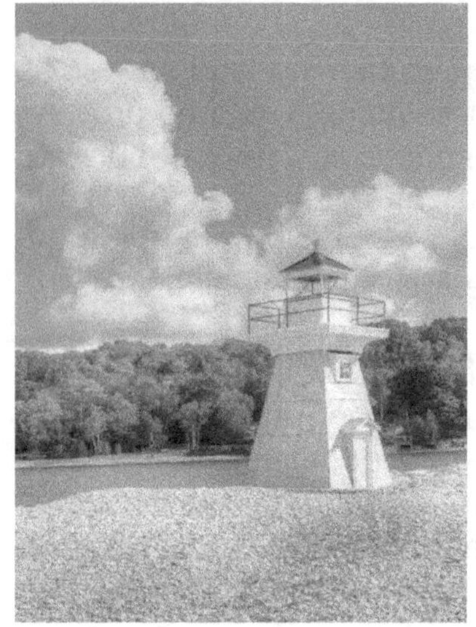

A lantern attached to a pole was the first light at Lion's Head on Georgian Bay in 1903. It was situated at the tip of the breakwater.

In 1913 a contract for a new lighthouse was fulfilled by J.C. Kennedy of Owen Sound who built a pyramid shaped tower on the breakwater. In November the Great Storm of 1913 hit the Great Lakes, the worst storm ever recorded there with 19 ships destroyed and the loss of over 250 crew. The Lion's Head Lighthouse was knocked off it's foundation by the hurricane force winds but was recovered and repaired. However in 1969, the Canadian Coast Guard declared the lighthouse unsafe and beyond repairs, and dismantled and destroyed it.

The lighthouse would return from the dead. In 1983 the Bruce Peninsula District School students took on a project of building a replica with financial help from the Lion's Head Rotary Club. The Coast Guard decided to make it functional. However after this was completed, a storm in 2020 badly damaged it. By September of that year, local volunteers had repaired it. It was moved somewhat to lessen its exposure to storms.

Description: Yellow tower with red corners and upper portion

Location: Lion's Head

Directions: On the Bruce Peninsula, head east on Bruce Rd 9/Bruce County Rd 9 from Highway 6 for 3 km. and turn left onto Main St/County Rd 29. In 0.9 km turn right onto Scott St and shortly, turn left at the 1st cross street onto Helen St and then a quick right onto McNeil St. where you will find the lighthouse.

Coordinates: 44°59'26.2"N 81°14'53.8"W

Opened: 1983 (Made functional in 2000)

Automated: 2000

Deactivated: Active

Height: 28 feet, (8.6 metres)

Focal Height: 26 feet (8 metres)

Signal: White. 2 seconds on, 2 seconds off

Visitor Access: Grounds open, interior closed

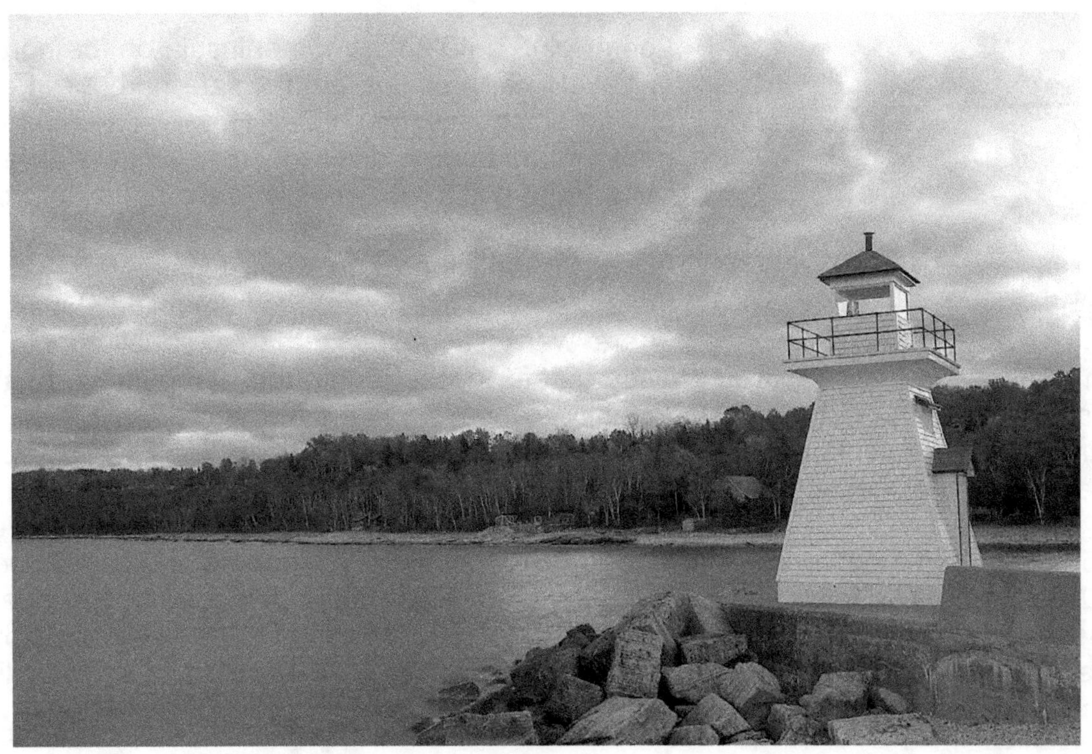

Long Point Cut Lighthouse, Southwestern Region

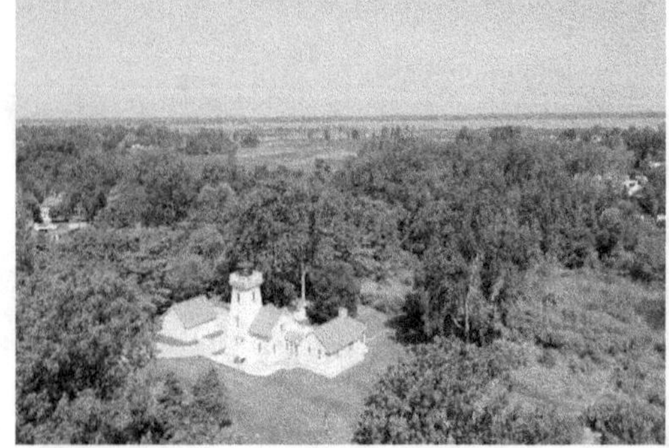

Long Point, a 40 km. long peninsula on the north shore of Lake Erie, provides both a safe harbour in it's inner bay for ships seeking shelter. However, getting into that harbour had been a different story, and the area around Long Point has been a ship's graveyard with more than 400 wrecks documented there, many at the tip of Long Point. In 1843 the Long Point Lighthouse was built at the entrance to the harbour to help guide ships safely in. There were suggestions that a canal should be cut through the base of Long Point to provide a safer passage into the harbour. When a natural canal formed in 1833, it was an opportunity to use it for this entrance. Piers were built to maintain the natural passage and in 1940, a lightship was positioned nearby but was moved elsewhere when the channel filled in.

In 1865 a storm created a new cut, and in 1878 parliament tendered a contract for a new lighthouse to mark this entrance. In 1879, the Long Point Cut Lighthouse began operations. After the cut filled in, it was deactivated in 1919. In 1999, the lighthouse was owned privately, and the owners had it restored in what was recognized as Most Outstanding Historical Restoration in Ontario for the year.

Description: White rectangular tower with red upper portion

Location: Long Point

Directions: At Long Point, take Erie Blvd/Hwy 59 east until just past Lighthouse Crescent and the lighthouse is on the left side.

Coordinates: 42°34'54.1"N 80°23'47.3"W

Opened: 1879

Deactivated: 1919

Lens: Catoptric

Height: 56 feet (17 metres)

Focal Height: 108 feet (33 metres)

Signal: Fixed red

Visitor Access: Privately owned, grounds and interior closed. Easy views from public road.

Long Point Lighthouse, Southwestern Ontario Region

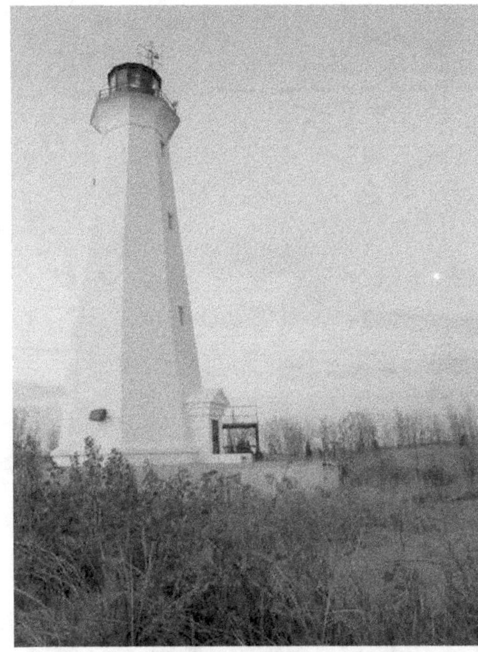

Long Point has been a graveyard for over 400 ships, more than the Bermuda Triangle. The area is sometimes termed "The Long Point Triangle" During violent storms ships often seek safety in the calmer waters of the Inner Bay. The shifting sandbars would often result in beaching of ships. While the bay could provide safety during the day, it was very dangerous to try to find the entrance at night.

This situation left many in the shipping business to ask for building of a lighthouse at the mouth of the Bay. The government of Upper Canada budgeted funds to build the first Long Point Lighthouse. The plans called for a circular, tapering stone tower of fifty feet and was contracted to Joseph, Benjamin, and Whitney Van Norman. By November, 1830 the project had progressed enough to light the building and the entire project was finished by the middle of 1831.

Problems arose by 1832 caused by erosion of the tower and Keeper's dwelling during storms. By 1838 inspections showed then structure in immediate danger of collapse. The Lighthouse was dismantled and moved inland and the dwelling was rebuilt in a safer position as well. It was all for naught. In 1943 a new wooden lighthouse and keeper's dwelling was built, a white octagonal structure of sixty feet.

A foghorn was added in 1906 which sounded for seven seconds with an interval of 30 seconds.

Long Point is a prime areas for bird migration and studies showed that large numbers of birds were being killed at the tower. Changes in the type and intensity of the light drastically reduced this number.

Description: White octagonal wood

Location: Long Point Provincial Park tip

Directions: Accessible by boat.

Coordinates: 42°32'55.5"N 80°02'57.6"W

Opened: 1916

Automated: 1990

Deactivated: Active

Lens: Solar-powered beacon

Height: 97 feet (29.6 metres)

Focal Height: 102 feet (29.6 metres)

Signal: White flash every eight seconds

Foghorn signal; Seven seconds with an interval of 30 seconds

Visitor Access: Grounds open, interior closed

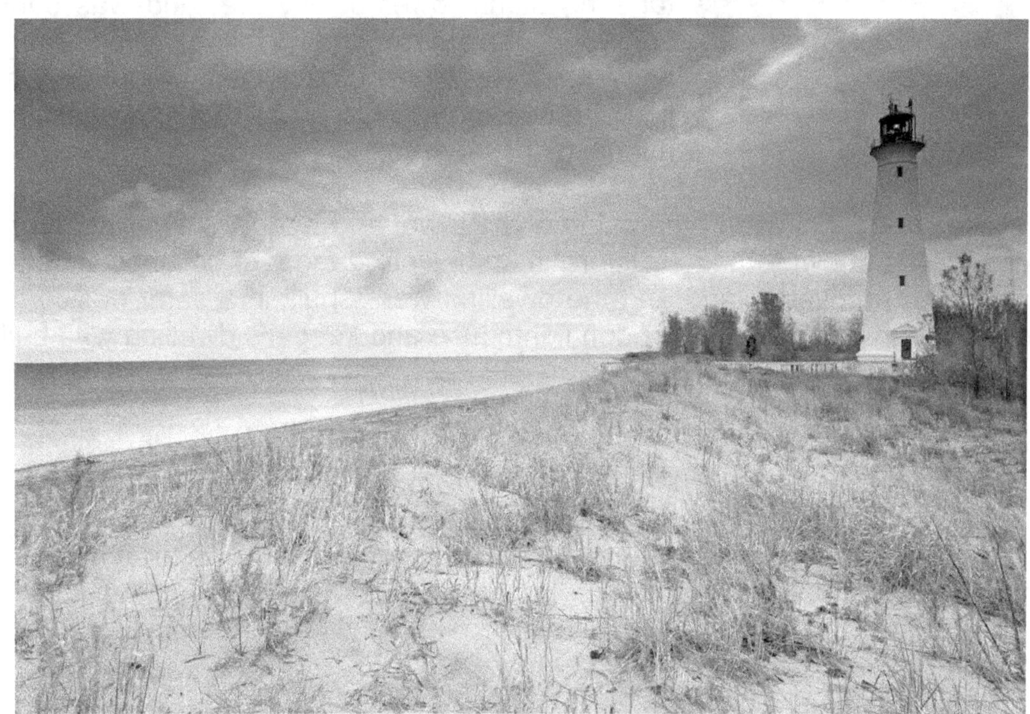

Pelee Island Lighthouse, Southwestern Ontario Region

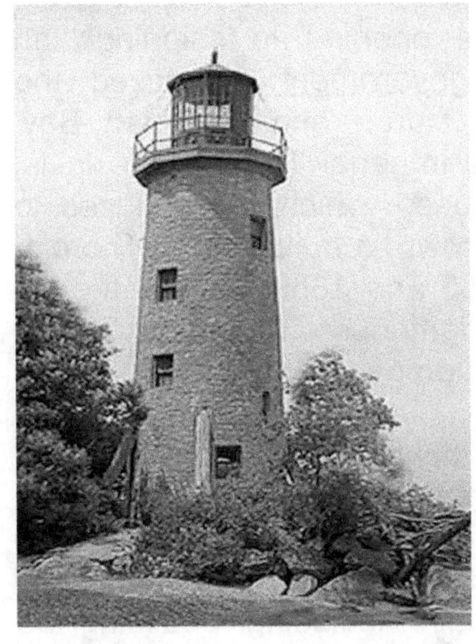

In 1833, John Scott of Detroit won a contract to build a lighthouse on the north tip of Pelee Island. He completed it successfully and the Pelee Island Lighthouse opened in October of 1933.

W. McCormick, who was the owner of Pelee Island donated land for the station, as well as stone for the tower. He eventually became the first Keeper of the lighthouse.

The fourth keeper, James Quick, was awarded a gold watch in recognition of his bravery in saving mariners in very dangerous conditions.

In 1908 A fifth-order Fresnel lens upgraded the lighting. However the station was deactivated the next year, as it was thought it was unnecessary due to the operation of the Pelee Passage Lighthouse. Funds were found to restore the lighthouse and it was completed by 2000.

Description: White cylindrical stone tower

Location: Pelee Island

Directions: Ferry from Leamington and Kingsville, Ontario and Sandusky, Ohio

Coordinates: 41°49'54.4"N 82°38'22.5"W

Opened: 1833

Deactivated: 1909

Lens: Fifth-order Fresnel

Height: 39 feet (12 metres)

Signal: Fixed red

Visitor Access: Ground open, interior closed

Point Clark Lighthouse, Southwestern Region

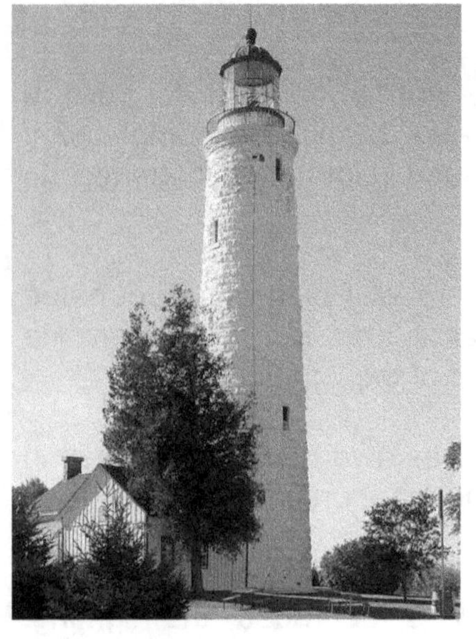

As the upper Great Lakes was opening to shipping and commerce in the 1850s, the government authorized the building of lighthouses at Lake Huron and Georgian Bay. These came to be known as the Imperial Towers. The initial contract called for eleven lighthouses, which was reduced to six due to cost increases. John Brown, a builder from Thorold, fulfilled this contract between 1855 and 1859. One of the six lighthouse is the Point Clark Lighthouse. There is further information on the Imperial Towers on page 9.

The Lighthouse was automated in 1925 but pressure from shipping resulted in reversing that decision. It would be 1962 before it became automated again. The lighthouse was listed as a National Historic site in 1966. The station was restored in 2011. This involved extensive repairs, including rebuilding the exterior of the tower. It was completed in 2014.

Description: White cylindrical tower

Location: Point Clark

Directions: From Highway 21, go northwest on Concession Rd 2 toward S Baseline for 4.1 km. and take a slight left onto Huron Rd. After 0.6 km. turn right onto Lighthouse Rd where you will find the lighthouse.

Coordinates: 44°04'22.1"N 81°45'26.3"W

Opened: 1859

Automated: 1962

Lens: Second-order Fresnel

Height: 87 feet (26.5 metres)

Focal Height: 93 feet (28.3 metres)

Signal: Fixed white flash every 10 seconds

Foghorn Signal: Short blast every 10 seconds

Visitor Access: Grounds open, interior open late June to Labour Day

Port Burwell Lighthouse, Southwestern Region

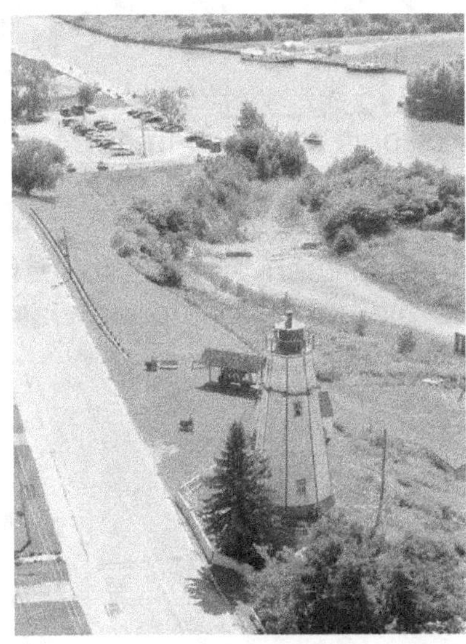

In 1837 the Upper Canada Assembly voted £500 to fund a lighthouse to be built in Port Burwell. Built in 1840 by Alexander Saxon, the Port Burwell Lighthouse is the oldest lighthouse surviving on Lake Erie. Care of the building has been primarily associated with the Sutherland family, 6 of whose members have served as Keepers.

The local community raised funds for a restoration of the structure. This was completed by Mennonite workmen in 1986, using hand tools that were comparable to the original ones used.

You can visit the pier just south of here to see the Port Burwell Entrance Lighthouse.

The building can be visited with admission charge from mid-May to Labour Day, open daily from 10:00 am - 5:30 pm. It was listed by the Canadian Register for its heritage value on July 23, 2007. The lighthouse is administered by the Port Burwell Marine Museum whose premises are across the street. In the immediate area, the submarine, HMCS Ojibwa, is also available to visit.

Location: Port Burwell

Directions: 20 Pitt St., Port Burwell

Coordinates: 42°38'41.0"N 80°48'21.0"W

Opened: 1840

Automated: 1962

Deactivated: 1962

Lens: Fourth-order Fresnel (added 1910)

Height: 45 feet (13.7)

Focal Height: Since the lighthouse stands on a hill, the focal height is 90 feet (27 metres)

Visitor Access: From mid-May to Labour Day (September): Open from 10:00 am - 5:30 pm

Port Dover Lighthouse, Southwestern Ontario Region

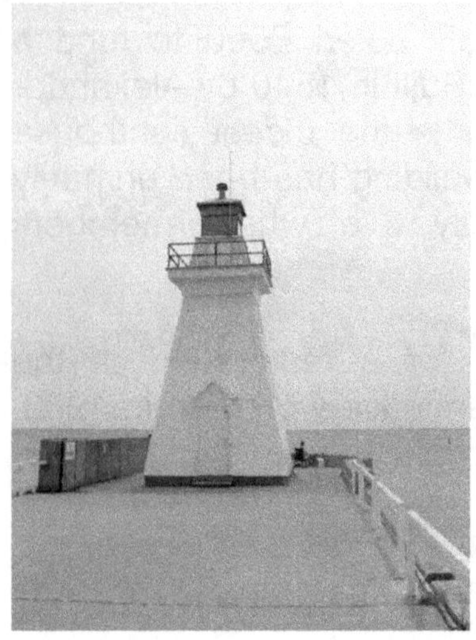

Port Dover's first lighthouse opened in 1845 but was destroyed in a fire in 1848. A second lighthouse was built in 1877. In 1904, it was removed for the current lighthouse which opened in 1905.

When visiting the lighthouse, have a look at the Memorial to lost mariners, found at the entrance to the pier. The lighthouse was recognized as a Historic Place on November 2, 2014.

Description: White square tower, green upper portion
Location: Port Dover

Directions: From Main St. in Port Dover, head southwest on Walker St for 01 km. Turn left onto St George St and in 0.1 km turn right onto Harbour St where the lighthouse is at the tip of the pier

Coordinates: 42°46'52.0"N 80°12'06.6"W

Opened: 1905

Automated: 1924

Deactivated: Active

Lens: Dioptric of the seventh order

Height: 36 feet (11 metres)

Focal Height: 37 feet (11.2 metres)

Signal: Green flash every 4 seconds

Foghorn Signal: 3 second blast twice a minute

Visitor Access: Grounds open, interior closed

Port Maitland Lighthouse, Southwestern Ontario Region

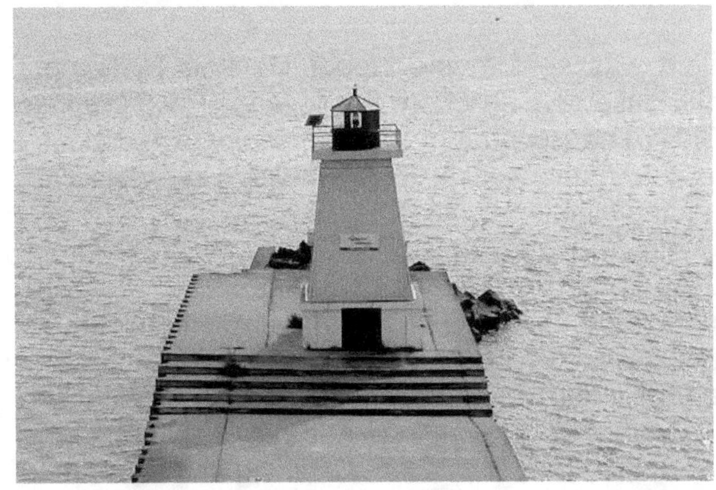

In 1846 a lighthouse was opened at the mouth of the Grand River. By 1870, an inspection showed the structure to be in very poor condition as was the pier it was on. Since repairs were too costly, a new lighthouse was built and opened in 1871. However it was destroyed in a fire in April of 1875.

The present lighthouse was built and opened by October, 1875. Initially it was an open frame structure with the lantern room on top but in 1927 the sides were enclosed. In 1911, a fourth-order Fresnel lens was added. The light was automated in the late 1930's.

Description: White square tower, green upper portion

Location: Port Maitland

Directions: From the town of Dunnville, head southwest on Rainham Rd/Haldimand 3 for 1 km. and turn left onto Port Maitland Rd/Regional R 11. In 5.9 km turn left to stay on Port Maitland Rd and in 1.1 km you will see the pier and the lighthouse.

Coordinates: 42°51'10.7"N 79°34'47.3"W

Opened: 1875

Automated: Ca. 1938

Deactivated: Active

Lens: Fourth-order Fresnel

Height: 41 feet (12.5 metres)

Focal Height: 50 feet (15.1 metres)

Signal: Green Light flashing every 4 seconds

Visitor Access: Grounds open, interior closed

Thames River Range Rear Lighthouse, Southwestern Ontario Region

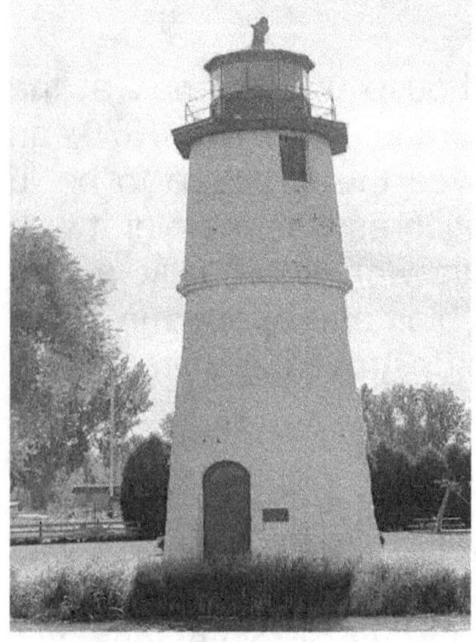

In 1837 a petition was sent to the Upper Canada Parliament asking that a lighthouse be built where the Thames River empties into Lake St. Clair. The government budgeted for a lighthouse there as well as for lighthouses at Port Burwell, Port Colborne, Oakville and Presque Island.

The Thames River Range Rear Lighthouse opened in 1837 and from that time until 1950, the lighthouse was associated with the Carter family. Claude Carter was the first Keeper and five other members of the family subsequently served as Keeper. After the Lower Thames Valley Conservation Authority obtained the lighthouse on 1972, they rehabilitated the building and it resumed operations in 1974.

Description: White cylindrical tower with red upper portion

Location: Tilbury

Coordinates: 42.317514°N 82.453297°W

Directions: Directions: From Tilbury, head north on Chatham-Kent County Rd 1 for 1.2 km and turn left onto Clouthier St/Lakeshore Rd 303/Concession Rd 3. After 2.1 km, turn right onto Big Creek Rd and continue another 1.4 km. Turn left onto Tecumseh Rd/County Rd 2 and in 0.9 km turn right onto Lighthouse Side Rd/County Rd 39. In 3.5 km. Continue onto Tisdelle Dr and make a slight right onto Lakeside Dr where you will find the lighthouse.

Opened: 1837

Automated: 1966

Deactivated: Active

Lens: Fifth-order Fresnel

Height: 54 feet (16.5 metres)

Focal Height: 52 feet (16 metres)

Signal: Fixed Red

Visitor Access: Grounds open, interior closed

Other Southwestern Region Lighthouses

Name: Colchester Reef

Description: Skeletal tower
Directions: Accessible by boat
Automated: 1954
Lens: Dioptric light of the third order
Focal Height: 71 feet (21.6 metres)
Access: Grounds open, interior closed
Coordinates: 41°55'56.6"N 82°53'31.5"W
Location: Colchester Reef
Opened: 1954
Deactivated: Active
Height: 41 feet (12.4 metres)
Signal: Red flash every 4 seconds

Name: Corunna Range Rear

Description: White square tapered tower
Directions: 94 Moore Line, Mooretown
Automated: 1948
Lens: Fifth-order Fresnel
Focal Height: 69 feet (20.7 metres)
Coordinates: 42°50'26.7"N 82° 27'44.8"W
Location: Mooretown
Opened: 1892
Deactivated: 1982
Height: 42 feet (12.8 metres)
Access: Grounds open, interior closed

Name: Goderich Breakwater

Description: White square tower
Directions: On W. end of S. breakwater
Automated: 1952
Focal Height: 34 feet (10.3 metres)
Access: Closed
Coordinates: 43°44'47.8"N 81°44'14.4"W
Location: Goderich
Opened: 1952
Deactivated: Active
Signal: Red 2 sec. Flash, 2 sec. eclipse

Name: Kingsville

Description: White square skeleton tower
Directions: Park St & Loop's Lane, Kingsville
Automated: 1925
Height: 16 feet (4.8 metres)
Signal: Fixed green
Coordinates: 42°01'39.2"N 82°44'10.7"W
Location: Kingsville
Opened: 1889
Lens: Reflector
Focal Height: 21 feet (6.5 metres)
Access: Grounds open, interior closed

Name: Leamington

Description: White square tapered tower
Directions: 36 Gold Coast Rd, Leamington
Automated: 1923
Lens: Forth-order Fresnel
Coordinates: 42°01'49.1"N 82°36'11.4"W
Location: Leamington
Opened: 1889
Deactivated: 1923
Access: Closed

Name: McNab Point
Coordinates: 44°28'18.8"N 81°23'32.6"W
Description: Square wooden tapered tower
Location: Port Elgin
Directions: 44 Bayview Point, Port Elgin
Opened: 1877
Automated: 1923
Deactivated: 1989
Lens: Catoptric
Height: 28 feet (8.5 metres)
Focal Height: 34 feet (10.3 metres)
Signal: Fixed white
Foghorn Signal: 2 blasts every minute
Access: Closed

Name: Midland Point Range Front
Coordinates: 44°47'12.4"N 79°51'56.9"W
Description: Square wooden tapered tower
Location: Penetanguishene
Directions: From Penetanguishene, head southeast on Fuller Ave for 1.2 km and turn left onto Midland Point Rd. In 3.4 km turn left onto Islandview Ln where you find the lighthouse
Opened: 1900
Automated: 1938
Deactivated: 1990s
Lens: Dioptric of the seventh order
Height: 34 feet (10.3 metres)
Access: Closed

Name: Midland Point Range Rear
Coordinates: 44°47'13.7"N 79°52'02.9"W
Description: Square wooden tapered tower
Location: Penetanguishene
Directions: From Penetanguishene, head southeast on Fuller Ave for 1.2 km and turn left onto Midland Point Rd. In 3.2 km turn left and the lighthouse is on the left in 0.2 km.
Opened: 1913
Automated: 1938
Deactivated: 1990s
Lens: Reflector
Height: 43 feet (13.1 metres)
Focal Height: 41 feet (12.5 metres)
Access: Closed

Name: Nancy Island
Coordinates: 44°31'06.3"N 80°01'17.7"W
Description: Square wooden tapered tower
Location: Tower Island
Directions: Can view from 5th St, Wasaga Beach
Opened: 1967
Note: This is a replica of the Collingwood Outer Range Front Lighthouse which was built as a Centennial project
Access: Grounds and interior open

Name: Nottawasaga
Coordinates: 44°32'18.9"N 80°15'31.3"W
Description: Cylindrical white tower
Location: Nottawasaga Island
Directions: Accessible by boat
Opened: 1858
Automated: 1958
Height: 80 feet (24.4 metres)
Deactivated: 2003
Lens: Second-order Fresnel
Focal Height: 86 feet (26.2 metres)
Access: Closed

Name: Pelee Passage
Coordinates: 42°20'21.6"N 82°55'51.2"W
Description: Cylindrical white tower
Location: Windsor
Directions: 9230 Riverside Dr E, Windsor
Opened: 1902
Automated: 1959
Deactivated: 1975
Lens: Dioptric of the third order
Height: 66 feet (20 metres)
Focal Height: 75 feet (22.9 metres)
Signal: 2 white flashes every 8 seconds
Foghorn Signal: 7 sec blast, 45 sec eclipse
Access: Grounds open, interior closed
Note: In 1980 the lighthouse was reassembled at its present location in Windsor

Name: Pelee Passage New
Coordinates: 41°51'14.8"N 82°34'54.8"W
Description: White cylindrical, with helipad
Location: Middle Ground Shoal
Directions: Accessible by boat
Opened: 1975
Automated: 1975
Deactivated: Active
Height: 94 feet (28.6 metres)
Focal Height: 93 feet (28.3 metres)
Signal: White flash every 4 seconds
Access: Closed

Name: Point Edward Range
Coordinates: 43°00'09.3"N 82°24'59.2"W
Description: White cylindrical tower
Location: Point Edward
Directions: From Victoria Ave in Windsor, walk north on the Bluewater Bike Path for 0.3 km
Opened: 1959
Automated: 1959
Deactivated: Active
Height: 31 feet (9.5 metres)
Focal Height: 42 feet (12.7 metres)
Signal: Fixed Red
Access: Grounds open, interior closed

Name: Port Burwell Entrance
Coordinates: 42°38'23.0"N 80°48'25.5"W
Description: Concrete pyramidal tower
Location: Port Burwell
Directions: Head south on Chatham St from Hwy 42 for 1.2 km and find the light on pier
Opened: 1930
Automated: 1930
Deactivated: Active
Height: 24 feet (7.4 metres)
Focal Height: 34 feet (10.3 metres)
Signal: White flash every 4 seconds
Access: Grounds open, tower closed

Name: Port Stanley
Coordinates: 42°39'18.5"N 81°12'48.0"W
Description: White square tower
Location: Port Stanley
Directions: From George St, head south on William St. for 0.6 km, lighthouse is on the pier
Opened: 1909
Automated: 1937
Deactivated: Active
Lens: Catoptric
Height: 33 feet (10.1 metres)
Focal Height: 38 feet (11.5 metres)
Signal: 2 sec green flash, 3 second eclipse
Foghorn Signal: 2 sec blast every 15 sec
Access: Closed

Name: Rondeau East Pier
Coordinates: 42°15'21.5"N 81°54'25.9"W
Description: White square skeleton tower
Location: Erieau
Directions: In Erieau, head west on Highway 12 to the lakefront where you can see the light on the breakwater
Opened: 1905
Automated: 1947
Deactivated: Active
Height: 34 feet (10.5 metres)
Focal Height: 36 feet (11 metres)
Signal: Red flash every 4 seconds
Foghorn Signal: 3 blasts each minute
Access: Grounds open

Name: Rondeau West Breakwater
Coordinates: 42°15'11.2"N 81°54'31.5"W
Description: White square tower
Location: Erieau
Directions: In Erieau, head west on Highway 12 to the lakefront where you can see the light on the breakwater
Opened: 1912
Automated: 1940
Deactivated: Active
Height: 30 feet (9.2 metres)
Focal Height: 36 feet (11 metres)
Signal: 2 sec green flash, 3 sec eclipse
Access: Grounds open

Name: Saugeen River Range Front
Coordinates: 44°30'05.5"N 81°22'31.9"W
Description: White tower
Location: Southampton
Directions: From Highway 21, head west on S Rankin St for 0.5 km and see the lighthouse
Opened: 1903
Automated: 1977
Deactivated: Active
Lens: Fifth-order Fresnel
Height: 36 feet (11 metres)
Focal Height: 34 feet (10.4 metres)
Signal: Fixed green
Foghorn Signal: 3 sec blast every 20 sec
Access: Grounds open, interior closed

Name: Saugeen River Range Rear
Coordinates: 44°30'03.4"N 81°21'59.3"W
Description: White tower
Location: Southampton
Directions: From Highway 21, head just east on S Rankin St where you can see the lighthouse
Opened: 1903
Automated: 1977
Deactivated: Active
Lens: Reflector
Height: 33 feet (10.2 metres)
Focal Height: 66 feet (20 metres)
Signal: Fixed green
Foghorn Signal: 3 sec blast every 20 sec
Access: Grounds open, interior closed

Name: Southeast Shoal
Coordinates: 41°49'34.7"N 82°27'46.1"W
Description: White square tower
Location: Southeast Shoal off Point Pelee
Directions: Accessible by boat
Opened: 1927
Automated: 1974
Deactivated: Active
Lens: Reflector
Height: 61 feet (18.7 metres)
Focal Height: 70 feet (21.3 metres)
Signal: Flash 0.3 sec, eclipse 9.7 sec.
Access: Closed

Name: Stokes Bay Range Front
Description: White cylindrical tower
Directions: Accessible by boat
Automated: 1956
Lens: Catoptric
Focal Height: 31 feet (9.4 metres)
Access: Grounds open, interior closed
Coordinates: 44°58'01.6"N 81°23'25.8"W
Location: Knife Islands
Opened: 1904
Deactivated: Active
Height: 41 feet (12.6 metres)
Signal: Red flash every 4 seconds

Stokes Bay Range Rear
Description: White square skeleton tower
Directions: Accessible by boat
Automated: 2009
Height: 74 feet (22.6 metres)
Signal: Fixed red
Coordinates: 44°58'01.2"N 81°23'24.6"W
Location: Knife Islands
Opened: 2009
Deactivated: Active
Focal Height: 62 feet (19 metres)
Access: Grounds open, tower closed
Note: The original Rear Range was moved to Bruce County Museum after deactivation

Lake Erie Lighthouse Tour

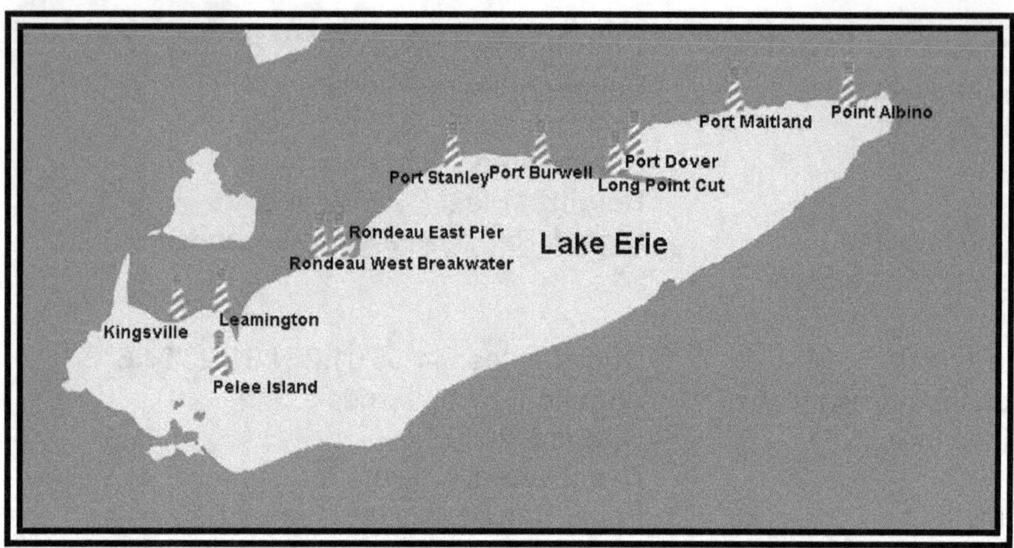

Following is an efficient order to visit eleven lighthouses on Lake Erie

Point Abino	42°50'07.7"N 79°05'42.7"W
Port Maitland	42°51'10.7"N 79°34'47.3"W
Port Dover	42°46'52.0"N 80°12'06.6"W
Long Point Cut	42°34'54.1"N 80°23'47.3"W
Port Burwell	42.644722°N 80.805833°W
Port Stanley	42°39'18.5"N 81°12'48.0"W
Rondeau East Pier	42°15'21.5"N 81°54'25.9"W
Rondeau West Breakwater	42°15'11.2"N 81°54'31.5"W
Pelee Island	41°49'54.4"N 82°38'22.5"W
Leamington	42°01'49.1"N 82°36'11.4"W
Kingsville	42°01'39.2"N 82°44'10.7"W

If you want to visit Pelee Island Lighthouse, you will need to take a ferry from Leamington, 500 Erie Street South, running from April until the end of July or from Kingsville, 25 Dock Rd from August until early December.

Total driving time is about 6 hours.

Golden Horseshoe Lighthouse Tour

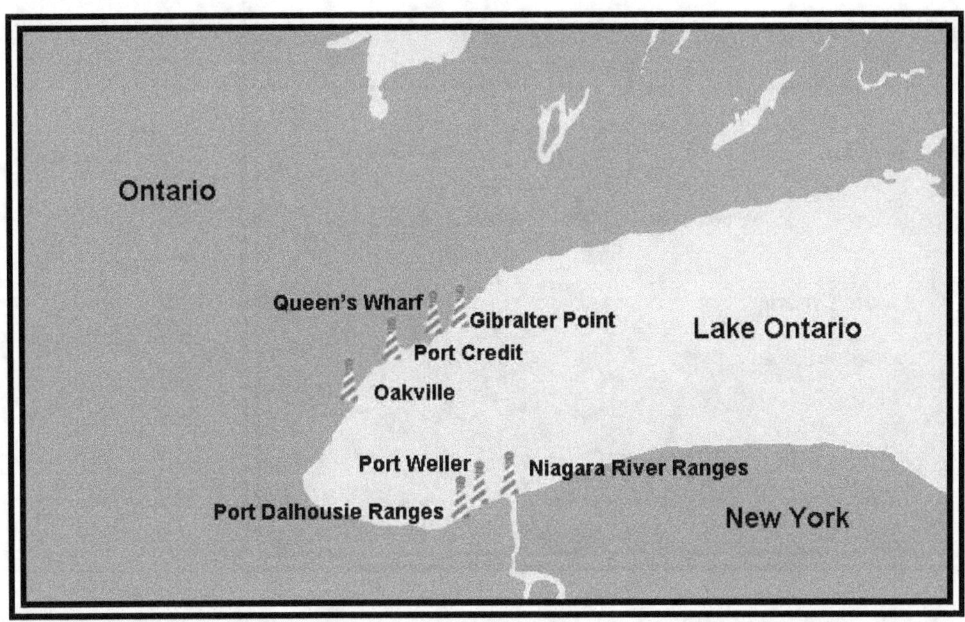

Following is an efficient order to visit nine lighthouses in the Golden Horseshoe area of Ontario,

Gibraltar Point	43°18'03.6"N 79°47'26.1"W
Queen's Wharf	43.635889°N 79.404972°W
Port Credit	43°33'01.3"N 79°35'09.8"W
Oakville	43°26'30.3"N 79°40'10.0"W
Port Dalhousie Range Front	43°12'39.9"N 79°15'48.6"W
Port Dalhousie Range Rear	43°12'25.2"N 79°15'44.0"W
Port Weller	43°14'41.2"N 79°13'03.2"W
Niagara River Range Front	43°15'19.7"N 79°03'42.4"W
Niagara River Range Rear	43°15'13.7"N 79°03'37.6"W

Gibralter Point Lighthouse is on Centre island in Toronto and is reached from the Jack Layton Ferry Terminal at 11 Queens Quay W. and taking the footpath southwest to the other side of the island.

The Port Dalhousie Ranges include the Port Dalhousie Range Front Lighthouse and the Port Dalhousie Range Rear Lighthouse. The Niagara River Ranges include the Niagara River Range Front Lighthouse and the Niagara River Range Rear Lighthouse.

The Port Weller Lighthouse is reached by the Pier Trail from the parking lot. It is 1.6 km. In length and is a quiet picturesque walk or bike.

Driving time is about 2.5 hours, depending on traffic.

Lake Ontario Lighthouse Tour

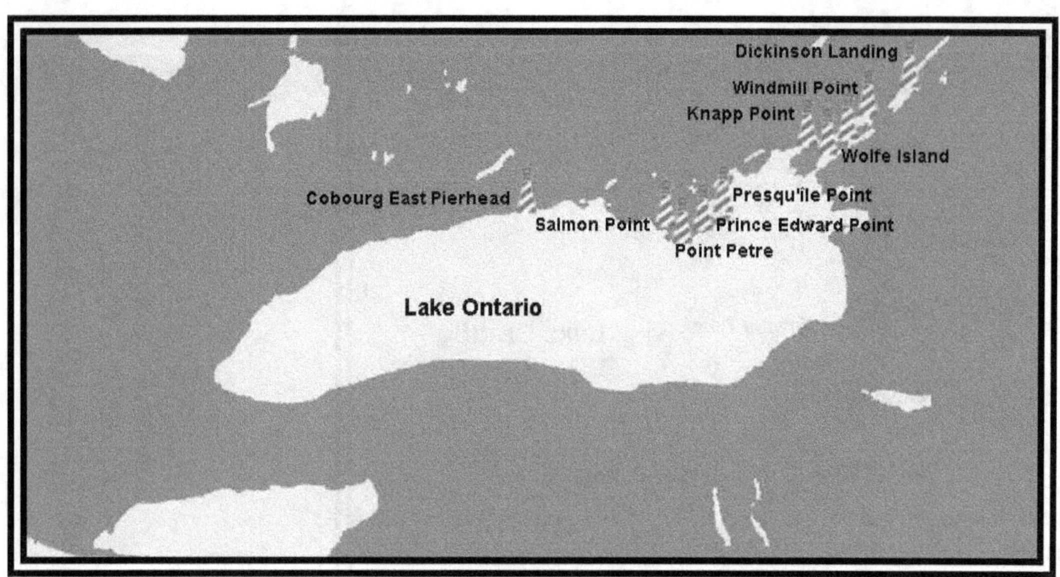

Following is an efficient order to visit nine lighthouses on Lake Ontario and the St Lawrence River

Cobourg East Pierhead	43°57'09.4"N 78°09'52.6"W
Salmon Point	43°51'25.4"N 77°14'39.4"W
Point Petre	43°50'25.1"N 77°09'07.2"W
Prince Edward Point	43°56'14.2"N 76°51'32.0"W
Presqu'île Point	43°59'52.1"N 77°40'38.3"W
Knapp Point	44°13'56.4"N 76°23'51.9"W
Wolfe Island	44°14'19.9"N 76°11'02.8"W
Windmill Point	44°43'15.3"N 75°29'13.7"W
Dickinson Landing	44°56'39.8"N 75°03'59.4"W

Knapp Island Lighthouse and Wolfe island Lighthouse are located on Wolfe Island. You can take the Wolfe Island Ferry Terminal, 295 Ontario St, Kingston, Ontario, Canada.

Wolfe Island Lighthouse is also known as Québec Head Lighthouse.

Total driving time is about seven hours.

Manitoulin Island Lighthouse Tour

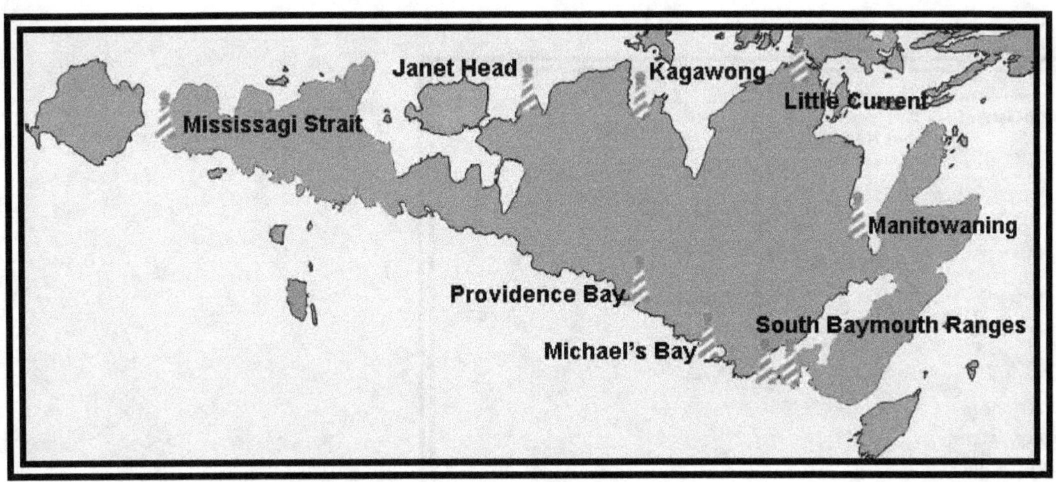

Following is an efficient order to visit nine lighthouses on Manitoulin Island

South Baymouth Range Front	45°33'27.7"N 82°00'47.9"W
South Baymouth Range Rear	45°33'33.1"N 82°00'44.6"W
Michael's Bay	45°34'35.4"N 82°07'40.0"W
Providence Bay	45°39'05.0"N 82°16'32.0"W
Mississagi Strait	45°53'29.5"N 83°13'32.5"W
Janet Head	45°56'45.0"N 82°28'48.6"W
Kagawong	45°54'35.6"N 82°15'37.4"W
Little Current	45°58'49.9"N 81°55'20.1"W
Manitowaning	45°44'41.4"N 81°48'18.5"W

Total driving time is about five hours. If you want to reduce this, you can skip the Mississagi Straits Lighthouse which reduces the driving time to three hours.

Note that Janet Head Lighthouse is also known as the Gore Bay Lighthouse.

Lake Huron-Bruce Peninsula Lighthouse Tour

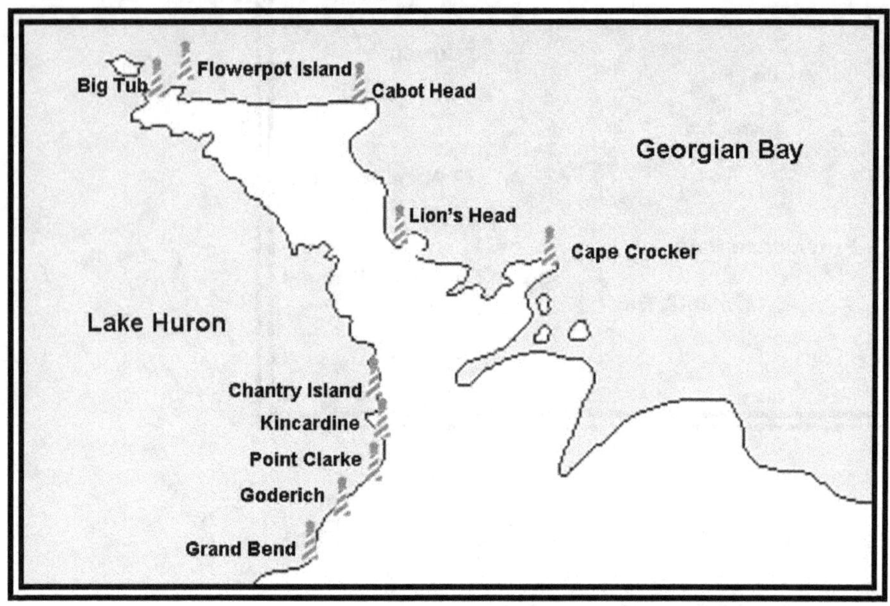

Following is an efficient order to visit ten lighthouses on the Lake Huron coast and the Bruce Peninsula.

Grand Bend	43.313820°N 81.768029°W
Goderich	43.742179°N 81.724564°W
Point Clark	44°04'22.3"N 81°45'26.0"W
Kincardine	44.17708°N 81.63809°W
Chantry Island	44°29'51.7"N 81°22'29.9"W
Big Tub	45°15'27"N 81°40'22"W
Flowerpot Island	45°18'25.9"N 81°36'49.6"W
Cabot Head	45°14'42.4"N 81°17'31.7"W
Lion's Head	44°59'26.2"N 81°14'53.8"W
Cape Croker	44°57'21.4"N 80°57'37.4"W

Total driving time is 5 hours 40 minutes and you will probably want to take more than one day if you plan to see all of the lighthouses.

Chantry Island is not accessible by car and the GPS position shown is for the beach at Southampton where you get a somewhat distant view.

You can visit the Lighthouse on Flowerpot Island by taking a Tour Boat from Tobermory. This is an excellent trip. The glass bottom boat visits the scene of several shipwrecks and the island is very picturesque with plenty of trails to explore. It also passes Big Tub Lighthouse, although you can visit it by car as well.

Glossary of Lighthouse Terms

Aerobeacon: A lighting system which creates a signal over long distances. It consists of a strong light source with a focusing mechanism which is rotated on a vertical axis. It has been used at airports as well as lighthouses.

Acetylene: After 1910, acetylene began to be used to power the lighthouse light source. It has the advantage that it could be stored on site with a sun valve turning it on at dusk and off at daybreak.

Alternating Light: A light source which changes colours in a regular pattern.

Arc of Visibility: The range of the horizon from which the lighthouse is visible from the sea.

Automated: A lighthouse that operates without a keeper. The light functions are controlled by timers, and light and fog detectors.

Beacon: A fixed aid to navigation.

Bell: A sound signal produced by fixed aids and by sea movement on buoys.

Breakwater: A structure that protects a shore area or harbour by blocking waves.

Bull's-eye Lens: A convex lens used to refract light.

Catwalk: An elevated walkway which allows the keeper to move in the lantern room in towers built in the sea.

Characteristic: The distinct pattern of the flashing light or foghorn blast which allows seamen to distinguish which light station it is coming from.

Chariot: A wheeled assembly at the bottom of a Fresnel lens which is rotated around a circular track.

Clockwork Mechanism: Early lighthouses had a series of gears, pulleys and weights, which had to be wound on a recurring basis by the keepers.

Cottage Style Lighthouse: A lighthouse made up of a keeper's residence with a light on top.

Crib: A base structure filled with stone which acted as the foundation for the structure built on top.

Daymark: A unique colour pattern that identifies a specific lighthouse during the day.

Decommissioned: A lighthouse that has discontinued operating as a aid to navigation.

Diaphone: A sound signal produced by a slotted piston moved by compressed air.

Directional Light: A light which marks the direction to be followed.

Eclipse: The interval between light flashed or foghorn blasts.

Fixed Light: A light shining continuously without periods of eclipse or darkness.

Flashing Light: Alight pattern distinguished by periods of eclipse or darkness.

Focal Plane: The path of a beam of light emitted from a lighthouse. The height from the center of the beam to the sea is known as the height of the focal plane.

Fog Detector: A device used to automatically determine conditions which may reduce visibility and the need to start a sound signal.

Fog Signal: An audible device such as a bell or horn that warns seamen during period of fog when the light would be ineffective.

Fresnel Lens: An optic system composed of a convex lens and prisms which concentrate the light beam through a series of prisms. The design was produced by Augustin Fresnel in the 1800s.

Geographic Range: The longest distance the curvature of the earth allows an object of a certain height to be seen.

Isophase Light: A light in which the duration of light and darkness are equal.

Keeper: The person responsible for the maintenance and operation of the lighthouse.

Lamp and Reflector: A lamp and polished mirror used before the invention of more effective optic systems such as the Fresnel lens.

Lantern: A glass covered space at the top of the lighthouse tower, which housed the lighting equipment.

Lens: The glass optical system used to concentrate and direct the light.

Light Sector: The arc over which a light can be seen from the sea.

Lightship: A ship that served as a lighthouse.

Light Station: The lighthouse tower as well as any outbuildings such as the keeper's quarters, fog-signal building, fuel storage building and boathouse.

Nautical Mile: A unit of distance which is the average distance on the Earth's surface represented by one minute of latitude. It is equal to 1.1508 statute miles and mainly used at sea.

Nominal Range: The distance a light can be seen in good weather.

Occulting Light: A light in which the period of light is longer than the period of darkness and in which the intervals of darkness are all equal. Also known as an eclipsing light.

Order: A description of the power of the Fresnel lens ranging from one to seven from stronger to weaker.

Parabolic Reflector: A metal bowl shaped to a parabolic curve which reflects a lamp's light from it's center.

Parapet: A railed walkway which surrounds the lamp room.

Period: The total time for one cycle of the pattern of the light or sound signal.

Pharologist: A person with an interest in lighthouses.

Range Lights: Two lights which form a range provide direction to mariners for safe passage. They are described as the Front and Rear Lighthouses or the Inner and Outer. The front range light is lower than the rear, and when they align,the ship is in the proper position.

Revetment: A bank of stone laid to protect a structure against erosion from waves.

Revolving Light: A flash produced by the rotation of a Fresnel lens.

Riprap: Broken rocks or stone placed to help prevent erosion.

Sector: The portion of the sea lit by a sector light.

Skeleton Tower: Towers consisting of four or more braced feet with a beacon on top. They have little resistance to the wind and waves, and bear up well in a storm.

Solar-powered Optic: Many automated lights are run on solar powered batteries.

Spider Lamp: A brass container holding oil and solid wicks.

Tender: A ship which services lighthouses.

Ventilator: Opening' at the top of a lighthouse tower to provide heat exhaust and air flow within the tower.

Wick Solid: A solid cord which draws fuel to the flame in spider lamps.

Photo Credits

Thank you to the following photographers who have provided images for this book. All other photographs are by the author.

Alessio Damato, A coruna torre de hercules, **Bpeninsula,** Cove Island, **Canadian Coast Guard,** Cape Croker, De Watteville Island Range, Deep River Islet , Janet Head , McQuestin Point, Michipicoten Island East End, Western Islands, **Charles Bash,** Victoria Harbour Range Rear, **Christopher Yaw,** Gros Cap Reefs, **Codell,** Mohawk Island, **D. Gordon E. Robertson,** Cape North, **David Bailey,** Killarney, **Dennis Jarvis,** Couburg East Pierhead, Dickinson Landing, Oakville, Prescott Heritage Harbour, Prescott, Sambro island, **Doug Kerr,** Goderich, **Duckminster,** Caribou Island, **Guerinf,** Cap-des-Rosiers, **Hermann Luyken,** Cabot Head, **James Hatcher,** Point Petre, **JethroElfman,** Port Dover**, JustSomePics,** Kincardine, **Laura Stanley,** Thunder Bay Main, Crocker **Library and Archives Canada,** Big Tub, Port Credit, **Marcus Obal,** Grand Bend, **Óðinn,** Presqu'ile Point, **Oxfordearl,** Manitowaning, **P199,** Mississagi Strait, **Padraic Ryan,** Gibraltar Point, **Peter Attfield,** Chantry Island, Gereaux Island, **Peter K Burian,** Chantry Island, **SimonP,** Queen's Wharf, **Susan Miller,** Battle Island, **Tim Mckee,** Point Clark, **Timothy Fenn,** Thames River, Toronto Harbour, **Vicki McKay,** Pointe au Baril, Snug Harbour, **Wbeard1,** Griffith Island, **Wpwatchdog,** Isle Parisienne, **Yoho2001 ,** Bois Blanc Island

Other Books by Harold Stiver

Unless noted, there are Print and eBook editions available for the following.

Birding Guide to Orkney

Ontario's Old Mills
Ontario Waterfalls
Ontario Lighthouses

Connecticut Covered Bridges (eBook only)
Delaware's Covered bridges (eBook only)
Georgia Covered Bridges (eBook only)
Indiana Covered Bridges
Maine Covered Bridges (eBook only)
Massachusetts Covered Bridges (eBook only)
Michigan Covered Bridges ((eBook only)
New England Covered Bridges
New Hampshire Covered Bridges
New York Covered Bridges
Ohio's Covered Bridges
The Covered Bridges of Kentucky (eBook only)
The Covered Bridges of Kentucky and Tennessee
The Covered Bridges of the Mid-Atlantic
The Covered Bridges of Tennessee (eBook only)
Vermont's Covered Bridges
The Covered Bridges of Virginia (eBook only)
The Covered Bridges of Virginia and West Virginia
The Covered Bridges of West Virginia (eBook only)

Index

Angus Island 67
Badgeley Island 11
Battle Island 57
Beausoleil Island 23
Big Tub 73
Bois Blanc Island 75
Brébeuf Island 23
Burlington Canal Main 41
Burlington Canal Pier 41
Bustard Rocks 23
Bustard Rocks Range 23
Byng Inlet Range Front 23
Byng Inlet Range Rear 23
Cabot Head 12
Cape Croker 13
Cape North 27
Cape Robert 24
Caribou Island 58
Cecebe Lake 24
Chantry Island 76
Christian Island 24
Cobourg East Pierhead 28
Colchester Reef 93
Coppermine Point 67
Corbeil Point 67
Corunna Range Rear 93
Cove Island 78
Davieaux Island 67
De Watteville Island Ranges 29
Deep River Islet 30
Dickinson Landing 31
False Ducks 38
False Ducks 1967 38
Flowerpot Island 14
French River Range 24
Gereaux Island 15
Giants Tomb Island 24
Gibraltar Point 43
Goderich 79
Goderich Breakwater 93
Gore Bay 61

Grand Bend 80
Gravenhurst Narrows 25
Great Duck Island 67
Griffith Island 16
Gros Cap Reefs 59
Ile Parisienne 60
Island No. 10 70
Janet Head 61
Jones Island Range Front 25
Jones Island Range Rear 25
Kagawong 62
Killarney East 17
Killarney Northwest 17
Kincardine 81
Kingsville, Leamington 93
Knapp Point 38
L'Orignal Range Front 38
L'Orignal Range Rear 38
Lamb Island 68
Lancaster Range 39
Lighthouse Island 25
Lighthouse Shoal 25
Lion's Head 82
Little Current 68
Lonely Island 68
Long Point 85
Long Point Cut 84
Main Duck 39
Manitowaning 63
McKay Island 68
McNab Point 93
McQuestin Point 32
Michael's Bay 68
Michipicoten Harbour 69
Michipicoten Island East End 64
Midland Point Range Front 94
Midland Point Range Rear 94
Mississagi Strait 65
Mohawk Island 44
Morris Island 39
Nancy Island 94
Niagara River Range Front 45

Niagara River Range Rear 45
Nine Mile Point 39
Nottawasaga 94
Oakville 47
Otter Island 69
Pelee Island 87
Pelee Passage 94
Pelee Passage New 95
Pie Island 69
Pigeon Island 39
Point Abino 48
Point Clark 88
Point Edward Range 95
Point Petre 33
Pointe au Baril Range Front 18
Pointe au Baril Range Rear 18
Pointe aux Pins Range Front 69
Pointe aux Pins Range Rear 70
Porphyry Point 70
Port Burwell 89
Port Burwell Entrance 95
Port Colborne Inner 56
Port Colborne Outer 56
Port Credit (replica) 50
Port Dalhousie Range Front 51
Port Dalhousie Range Rear 51
Port Dover 90
Port Maitland 91
Port Stanley 95
Port Weller 53
Prescott 35
Prescott Heritage Harbour 34
Presqu'île Point 36
Prince Edward Point 40
Providence Bay 70
Québec Head 40
Queen's Wharf 54
Red Rock 19
Rondeau East Pier 95
Rondeau West Breakwater 96
Rosseau 25
Salmon Point 40

Sand Point 40
Saugeen River Range Front 96
Saugeen River Range Rear 96
Scotch Bonnet Island 40
Shaganash 70
Shoal Island 70
Slate Islands 70
Snug Harbour Range Rear 20
South Baymouth Range Front 71
South Baymouth Range Rear 71
Southeast Bay 25
Southeast Shoal 96
Spruce Shoal 26
Stokes Bay Range Front 96
Stokes Bay Range Rear 96
Strawberry Island 71
Thames River Range Rear 92
Thunder Bay Main 66
Tobermory 73
Tomahawk Island 71
Toronto East Entrance Inner 56
Toronto East Entrance Outer 56
Toronto Harbour 55
Trowbridge Island 71
Victoria Harbour Range Rear 21
Victoria Island 39
Walton Island Range Front 20
Welcome Island 72
West Sister Rock 72
Western Islands 22
Wilson Channel Range Front 26
Wilson Channel Range Rear 26
Windmill Point 37
Wolfe Island 40

www.ingramcontent.com/pod-product-compliance
Lightning Source LLC
LaVergne TN
LVHW080322110826
845155LV00026B/184
9781927835289